WHAT OTHERS ARE SAYING ABOUT ELIAS KANARIS AND THIS BOOK

"Leveraging God may seem (as the author first states) blasphemous or even sacrilegious. But when the author is Elias Kanaris, you get a whole new meaning. This book shares a deeply personal journey with both philosophical and spiritual insights that you can apply immediately to your own life. It is both a guidebook and an instructional methodology to living your life. It uses an easy-to-read storytelling format to take you on a journey of discovery. I highly recommend taking your time to read this book."

John B. Molidor, Ph.D., CSP, Professor Emeritus, Psychiatry and Behavioral Medicine, Michigan State University - College of Human Medicine. Author of Crazy Good Interviewing: How Acting A Little Crazy Can Get You The Job

"Elias Kanaris does it again! I thoroughly enjoyed his book, Liberating Your Leadership Potential, and had the pleasure of completing a book study with him. The lessons shared in that book shaped me not only in business but in my personal life. In Leveraging God, Elias helps us to turn our focus on the fact that God is always there for us. What many say is just luck or good fortune is God working on our behalf. Elias writes a fantastic reminder of the love our Creator has for us and what can and will happen when we put our trust in Him and follow His lead. This book is a fantastic list of examples and steps to take in your faith to unlock all that God has planned for you."

Jennifer Dotzert, Area Manager with Arbonne

"In reading Elias' latest book, I'm reminded of the quote attributed to Leonard Ravenhill 'A man with an experience of God is never at the mercy of a man with an argument.' As constructive and beneficial as many of the technical aspects of this book may be, it will be Elias' own personal journey and associated anecdotes that are most likely to encourage you. Read and be inspired!!"

> Glen Sharkey - Director of the Lifeworks Co Ltd., Certified Speaking Professional, Multi-award winning speaker, facilitator and author, Immediate Past President of Professional Speakers NZ

"This book is very much like sitting beside Elias and chatting with him. It is a testimony of how he stepped up when opportunities were presented. Miracles can happen every day when we step out of the boat when Jesus calls us. There are keys to handling financial crises and choosing to learn from adversity and not let it define you. Elias is a man of integrity and has an openness and teachability in the different jobs he chose to do. I think this is because money was not the goal but a tool to be used. I would highly recommend this book to anyone who wishes to fly with what talents God has given you and learn to succeed in life."

> Jan Morris, Auckland

"I have always considered myself agnostic – I have witnessed things that can't be explained by what I can see and touch, but I certainly have felt that a 'great spirit' exists. The place I find myself most in touch with my spirituality is while flying, so it is fitting that I found myself reading the majority of this book while flying back to New Zealand! In the two years that I have known Elias his strong belief in God has been very inspirational. This book has helped me reflect on my own life, and beliefs, and I am thankful that I have had a chance to read it".

> Dave Greenberg, Emergency Management Consultant and Speaker, Wellington, NZ

"Kindness is an essential principle for a leader to embody and is visible in this content. Elias Kanaris has a unique way to take you on an authentic journey to *see yourself in his examples and experiences. Elias is genuine and in a remarkable way weaves God's work and testimony through his writing, and provides food for thought for leaders at any stage in their career."*

Nancy L Kittridge, Executive Director of the John Maxwell Team and President/CEO of Kittridge Connection, Inc.

"A significant coach in my life once said to me, "Don't you worry Pat Armitstead, God's got your number!" And every time she said that the phone would ring!! My takeaway from reading the book was, irrespective of what our individual faith is in, when we are guided, listen and act, we will meet that which we are seeking!! Anybody who is looking to restore their faith or find hope will find direction in this story, because they will get to see what is already around them waiting to be noticed and received!"

Pat Armistead, Multi-Award Winning Speaker, Author and Radio Host and Past President National Speakers Association NZ

"I don't believe in anything but I do believe in Elias Kanaris' ability to write a compelling narrative. He says early on that even if you don't share his beliefs, you can benefit from reading his book. I don't and I did. I'm a cynic in a cynical world and it's refreshing to delve into the writings of someone with similar business and personal goals to myself but with a very different approach to achieving them. The author is not afraid to challenge his readers, indeed he doesn't seem afraid at all, to tell his stories and bring us along for several rollercoaster rides."

Terry Williams, People Engagement Expert

"I have known Elias for a long time and have witnessed many of his testimonies first-hand. As I read the book, I am reminded of how God can open and close doors demonstrating his favour and sovereignty on lives that are committed to living as per biblical principles and laws. Thank you, Elias, for your transparency and honesty, sharing the good and tough times on your journey to date. Thank you for continuing to pursue God with all your heart and I admire your desire to

raise leaders based on your real-life experiences and biblical learnings. The reader will take away biblical nuggets that they can apply and see their lives changed."

Stephen Armstrong, General Manager – International, CDB Group of Companies

"As Elias reveals his journey you find yourself also being led on an effortless path of self-discovery and heightened awareness. Be sure to grab a notepad so you can jot down your own revelations as you share in Elias' journey of insight and inspiration."

Francesca Hosking

"This book is not about Elias' accomplishments. It is full of real-world examples about how God accomplished things as Elias learned how to tap into His power and how He can do the same for you!"

Chris Rollins- President of Rollins Performance Group, Inc.

"Reading LEVERAGING GOD was as if Elias was speaking directly to my life story. I was hooked on reading more to see what happened next. Elias' journey to faith and keeping the faith is inspiring. Totally enjoyable."

Alan Tane Solomon – Coach, Trainer, Speaker, Enthusiast

"Reaching the inner self is a journey of reaching the authentic leadership. And this book is the compass."

Ayesha J Bibha – International Speaker, Mentor and Author of the upcoming book, "Mindspeed."

"This book resonated so well with my interests like property investment, global speaking, belief in human potential and we should be listening to inner voices and many more. I am sure it would help this world by nurturing many more leaders."

Vikas Jain – Author | Speaker | Entrepreneur

"Thank you for sharing your Journey of "leveraging" God while walking in His Grace and Power! Very seldom do we have the opportunity to read a story such as yours filled with transparency and hope! Every businessman should be able to relate and learn from your real life dilemmas. God bless you, Kay, and your sweet family."

Charles V. Christie – Founder, Ambassador Trust Corp.

"This latest leadership book by Elias is at an entirely new level of thinking. This is not a book you can only read once and think you have explored all the messages and meanings held within. No. This book has layers of thought-provoking insights, questions and illustrations that come straight from the real-life wins and losses of Elias's personal journey. There is no substitute for personal experience, and in this book, Elias bears his soul and tells his story. This book will challenge you to think about your relationship with God, yourself, your finances, your family and even your friends. I know this because that is exactly what happened to me when I read it. Thank you, Elias, for writing such an essential book."

Eugene Moreau, Author of Leaving Almost: The Journey of a Lifetime

"Elias eloquently tells his story from struggle to success with his faith in God. He is candid in his experiences and offers practical advice alongside scripture. If you are looking for strength to achieve your dreams and desires, this book will help – whatever your faith level."

Karen Tui Boyes CSP – Spectrum Education, Speaker, Author, Lifelong Learning Advocate.

LEVERAGING GOD

GIVING YOU STRENGTH TO HELP YOU ACHIEVE ANYTHING YOU DESIRE

ELIAS KANARIS

PUBLISHING
New York

Leveraging God:
Giving You Strength to Help You Achieve Anything You Desire

Copyright © 2020 by Elias Kanaris. All rights reserved.

Published by:
Aviva Publishing
Lake Placid, NY
(518) 523-1320
www.AvivaPubs.com

All Rights Reserved. No part of this book may be used or reproduced in any manner whatsoever without the expressed written permission of the author. Address all inquiries to:

Elias Kanaris
Phone: +64 9 280 4420
Email: info@EliasKanaris.com

www.LeveragingGod.com

ISBN: 978-1-950241-96-5 (paperback)
ISBN: 978-1-950241-97-2 (ePub)

Library of Congress:

Editor: Don Henderson/Kay Kanaris
Cover Designer and Interior Book Layout: Roland Meissner/Love Your Brand
Author Photo: Rory Laubscher/Firefly Photography

Every attempt has been made to source properly all quotes.

Printed in the United States of America

First Edition

2 4 6 8 10 12

DEDICATION

To my surrogate mum, Maureen Murfitt. You are an awesome prayer warrior not only for my family and me, but for the many others whom you've met. I want to thank you and acknowledge you for your inspiring faith, belief and support.

You were a blessing to my daughter Brianna, when you became her 'Warrior' at City Impact Church. Without any grandparents here in New Zealand, Brianna needed another voice in her life to guide her and show her the way. You not only became that voice, but you were a shining light that breathed life and life abundantly into me and my family.

You are generous. You are insightful. You are caring. And you are filled with the Holy Spirit. You see the best in people and you always intercede with prayers and messages of encouragement and hope. You have shown unfailing faith and you are known by the phrase, "I love my Jesus!"

I'm blessed to call you my surrogate mum and to have you in my life. In many respects, this book is about our journey together. Without God, it is impossible to accomplish anything. But through God, we get His strength, and anything is possible.

Thanks, Maureen, for being a large part of my life since 2010.

ACKNOWLEDGEMENTS

No book is written alone, so I would like to thank the many people who have influenced my journey:

Dr. John B. Molidor, Steven French, Jennifer Dotzert, Glen Sharkey, Jan Morris, Dave Greenberg, Nancy L Kittridge, Pat Armistead, Terry Williams, Stephen and Jalaine Armstrong, Francesca Hosking, Chris Rollins, Alan Tane Solomon , Ayesha J Bibha, Vikas Jain, Charles V. Christie, Eugene Moreau, Linda Guirey, Linda Rugg, Dr. John C. Maxwell, Paul Adams, Richie Lewis, Kary Oberbrunner, Pastor Peter Mortlock, Simon and Yvonne Godfrey, Karen Tui Boyes, Martin Brooker, Bavani Periasamy and Wynand Jacobs.

I would also like to thank five more people who were all very influential in making this project work. Don Henderson for his support and help in guiding me during the editing of this manuscript. Roland Meissner for his expertise in graphic design. You brought my vision of this book to life. Patrick Snow for his enthusiasm and support as my publishing coach. The Holy Spirit, who encouraged me to write the framework of this book in less than three weeks. And finally, my wife, Kay Kanaris, for your ability to proofread and edit this manuscript and allowing me to expose our inner secrets for the world to see. You were my biggest cheerleader, and without your expertise, this book may never have been birthed.

Contents:

	Foreword	17
	Introduction	21
Chapter 1	Are you making eye contact?	29
Chapter 2	What is your secret name?	39
Chapter 3	Why did Eve's bite affect me?	49
Chapter 4	Why is New Zealand the land of the long white underbelly?	55
Chapter 5	What does it take to go from zero to hero?	63
Chapter 6	Why is it relevant to connect to John Maxwell and The 21 Irrefutable Laws of Leadership?	73
Chapter 7	What is your calling?	87
Chapter 8	What does a free man do with his time?	99
Chapter 9	What is your burden?	107
Chapter 10	Are you working in your own strength?	121
Chapter 11	Why should you clean yourself with your daily S.O.A.P.?	129
Chapter 12	Is scripture more powerful than an airbag?	137
Chapter 13	Do you have the full picture?	143
Chapter 14	Why bother painting the town red?	155
Chapter 15	What are the unexpected benefits of leaving one job for another?	167
Chapter 16	What would you do if you woke up and found yourself $2,000,000 in debt?	179
Chapter 17	What is the writing on the wall?	187
Chapter 18	Are you ready to start bidding?	195
Chapter 19	Conclusion	203
	A Final Note: Strengthen yourself to achieve anything you desire	209
	About the Author	213
	About Executive Coaching	215
	Book Elias Kanaris to speak at your next event	217

FOREWORD

Who is Elias Kanaris and why should I bother reading this book?

Not all stories are created equal. Not all books are written exceptionally well, but when I picked up "Leveraging God", I was compelled to turn the page and keep reading...

This book stinks!

Or should I rather say this book is filled with the aroma of a life that gives evidence to the goodness of God and the "more" that is available to you if you're willing to lean into the promises of God.

I've come to know Elias as an influential leader in his field and it was no surprise to me when I learned that beneath his drive for excellence and genuine care for people is his faith in Christ. Since I believe in perfect timing, the title of this book also made a lot of sense to me as I'm writing this foreword in a season where the idea of "partnering with God" has been front of mind in my own devotional time and biblical meditation.

My first encounter with Elias was not in the Christian context, but at the professional speakers association. Elias, the president elect of the association, offered a ride to me, a stranger, which soon turned into a powerful prayer opportunity as he eloquently shares in Chapter 8. I've always admired Elias as a leader and when I was applying for the Executive Director role at FamilyLife I knew I had to sit down and have a conversation with him about it.

Fast forward to late 2019. I was appointed the position and Elias and I caught up for another coffee where we talked through what his next steps would be. There we were, sipping away at our flat whites and linking all the dots from past experiences in an attempt to decipher how it all connected.

In what seemed like an "aha" moment, the lights went on and Elias told me: "I know what comes next". The book you are holding in your hands is the result of a lifetime of experiences and seemingly random events that all came together in a defining moment where the calling became clear.

Not many people take the time to make sense of their lives and past events to recognise the journey they had been on and how God was ultimately interested in them and present with them through it all. When you recognise how the dots all connect to create this unique expression of God in the world, it's like music. Through this book, Elias took the time to reflect, connect the dots and his work will continue to inspire many leaders both within the faith context and outside.

> *"The whole creation waits breathless with anticipation for the revelation of God's sons and daughters."*
> (Romans 8:17, CEB)

One of the biggest criticisms of Christianity today is Christians. There are too many who call themselves "Christian" but they do not live a life consistent with the values Jesus displayed in his walk here on earth. It's sad to see so many reject a relationship with Christ on the basis of Christians who don't represent Him well. In Leveraging God, Elias not only displays what the Jesus journey looks like from a "love your neighbour" point of view, but he also shows what "living victoriously" looks like and how God wants you to achieve "exceedingly abundantly" more with Him than you could on your own.

Wherever you are on your faith journey, the easy to read and enjoyable stories shared by Elias in this book will encourage and perhaps even challenge you to take another step closer to your Creator. Why would you go at life alone when you could be "Leveraging God"?

What I enjoyed the most about carving out the time to read "Leveraging God" was the fact that I did not want to put it down. "Busyness" seems to be the buzz-word of the 21st century. Who has the time to sit down and read another book? Sometimes, however, you have to slow down to speed up and I'm glad I slowed down to read "Leveraging God".

Wynand Jacobs
Coach, Author, Speaker
Executive Director - FamilyLife NZ

INTRODUCTION

What would you do if you found yourself $2,000,000 in debt, with all your lines of credit maxed out? Would you call it quits? Would you call in the liquidators and declare bankruptcy? Would you rush around and see who you can persuade to loan you some money – any money? Family? Friends?

Or would you leverage God?

What??! Don't be sacrilegious, Elias. What you are saying is blasphemous. You can't manipulate God!

I'm not saying that I tried to manipulate God. I'm just saying that I was leveraging God. There's a subtle and important distinction...

By leaning into God and allowing myself to submit to His will and His word, I was able to remove 94% of my debt in less than six months. All legally. All above board. Without having to sell my home from beneath us. And all through Him and His strength.

If you think that this is a miracle, let me tell you that I saw an even bigger miracle unfold before my eyes between 2005 and 2007, when God dissolved $160,000 of debt in two years. I classify this as a bigger miracle because what I learned in the last six months of that period taught me everything that I needed to know about leveraging God.

If you are a Christian – whether you are a new believer, or you happen to be a mature person of faith – I encourage you to read this book. If you're not a person of faith, I still encourage you to read this book. If you're an atheist or agnostic, I encourage you to take a leap of faith and read this book.

Here's the bottom line – read this book!

Before you say anything else, let me share a little about two things:
1) Me, and
2) The concept of leveraging God.

First off, let me tell you my back-story. I grew up in a Christian (Greek Orthodox) family. My father was born in Jerusalem and my mother in Bethlehem. My mum used to tell me that we were from the same tribe as Jesus (no pressure there!).

I'm the youngest of three siblings and I was born in Tripoli, Libya. Life was idyllic growing up in one of the countries that we now know to be 'beyond the Axis of Evil' (https://en.wikipedia.org/wiki/Axis_of_evil). Idyllic, except for the fact that I was called an idiot by my father as I grew up. This didn't bode well for me and, allegedly, at the age of four or five, I turned around to my mum to ask her for a knife – so that I could stab dad in the back and kill him!

Of course, the constant re-enforcement of being called an idiot did eventually take its toll on me. I underachieved at school (I was bottom of my class). I self-sabotaged at work and in my career (I rarely held a role for more than two or three years). And I failed in my relationships (divorcing my first wife after less than six years of marriage).

Yet, despite these outward markers of failure, I found myself becoming the President of a Political Party in 2008 and heading up a US$4 Billion industry in 2018. As a man of faith, all I can say is that God saw something in me that I didn't see in myself!

Have I always been a man of faith? Not really.

At the age of 15, I found myself walking away from God. It took me nearly 30 years of walking in the wilderness before I returned to a relationship with Him. (I am glad that I must be a quicker leaner than the tribe of Israel who spent 40 years wandering in the wilderness!) I have always known that God was real and that He sent His Son to earth to die a cruel and painful death for my sins. But for thirty agonizing years, I chose to do it my way.

Everything changed for me the day I went to Church in January 2005 and accepted Jesus into my heart. I'd love for you to think that I became a perfect person overnight. But that wasn't the case. My transformation took me nearly 24 months. I had to shift from treating God as a religious experience to developing a relationship with Him. More will be explained as you read this book.

INTRODUCTION

Now, let me talk to you about the second concept: leveraging.

Leverage can be a noun or a verb.

As a noun, leverage is related to the action of a lever or the mechanical advantage gained by it. You can use a lever to create a larger force that can be used to your advantage. For example, think of using a stick and fulcrum to move a heavy rock. A lever works by reducing the amount of force needed to move an object or lift a load. A lever does this by increasing the distance through which the force acts.

As a verb, leverage can be related to using something that you already have in order to achieve something new or better. It is this concept that I want you to explore in this book.

An online definition of leveraging is to:

1. use borrowed capital for (an investment), expecting the profits made to be greater than the interest payable (for example, in "a leveraged takeover bid") or

2. use (something) to maximum advantage (for example, "the organization needs to leverage its key resources").

It is the second description that I'd like to investigate with you. And this starts off with the premise that I found myself debt-free, as a result of becoming diligent in following the teaching of Jesus Christ.

In this book, I will take you through the journey that I experienced and show you what I learned by way of reading my Bible and applying these principles within my life. I will explain the simplicity of what God has revealed to me and share with you some practical steps that you can take in your life. None of this is mumbo-jumbo. This is the reality of what my wife, Kay, and I experienced.

This book is not a self-help book. It is about giving you strength to help you achieve anything you desire. This is a self-leadership road map of personal transformation.

In this book, you will learn that:

- God can do anything
- You are made in the image of God
- If you follow God's blueprint, you can accomplish miracles

- The word 'BIBLE' stands for **B**est **I**nstruction **B**efore **L**eaving **E**arth
- It is His timing, not your timing
- He has a plan for you
- Your Given Name does not have to define your identity
- You have a Secret Name that defines your true identity
- You can serve a prayer-answering God
- You have to have faith
- God knows your every need and will provide everything that you need
- You have to be a good steward of what you have been given
- If you try things in your own strength, you will probably fail
- You can have a relationship with God
- God is not a religious experience
- Anything is possible in God
- Obedience will be rewarded
- Irrespective of what your past is, God is willing to wipe the slate clean and help you start over

As I said, if you apply the wisdom offered in this book, you will start leveraging God by giving you strength to help you achieve anything you desire.

Despite my disastrous academic record, I invested in my personal development and read many self-help books and inspirational autobiographies. One in particular, the Bible, the world's best-selling book, impacted me more than any other. Whilst all the books that I have read have helped me to change my personal outlook, I want to draw some lessons from the Bible and Jesus' life that you can apply to your individual journey.

Maybe, like me, you have been stuck in a jail of self-limiting beliefs. Maybe you have had a false identity applied to your life through a Given Name that you have received. Maybe you aspire to achieve more, but you simply cannot find the keys to unlock the doors that have imprisoned you. Maybe, like me, you need to review your thinking and determine how it can affect your ambitions.

We live in a world that is noisy. The message that needs to get through to you can be drowned out by many things that can easily distract you. Trust me when I tell you that God has been trying to speak to you, but you just haven't

INTRODUCTION

been able to hear His voice.

In the Old Testament, there is a story that talks about God's Revelation to Elijah:

> "*11 Then He said, "Go out, and stand on the mountain before the Lord." And behold, the Lord passed by, and a great and strong wind tore into the mountains and broke the rocks in pieces before the Lord, but the Lord was not in the wind; and after the wind an earthquake, but the Lord was not in the earthquake; 12and after the earthquake a fire, but the Lord was not in the fire; and after the fire a still small voice. 13So it was, when Elijah heard it, that he wrapped his face in his mantle and went out and stood in the entrance of the cave. Suddenly a voice came to him, and said, "What are you doing here, Elijah?"'*
> (1 Kings 19:11-13, NKJV)

After reading these words, I was able to hear God's voice. And what He said to me helped me to let my insecurities and self-limiting beliefs go. Maybe, like me, you can let yours go and accomplish more for your life, your business, your team, or even your country.

Don't let the strong wind, nor the earthquake, nor the fire distract you. Listen out for the small voice. My prayer is that by reading this book, you will start to hear that still, small voice.

I have held senior roles in the financial services, information technology, and telecommunications sectors. I was the senior consultant in the largest Telco here in New Zealand, working within a team responsible for the top twenty-four trans-Tasman customers with a combined billing of over $450 million per annum. I became the party president for a political party that contested the 2008 General Election in New Zealand, with overall responsibility for a 300+ strong volunteer workforce. As a founding partner of the John Maxwell Team, I was one of the first members invited to join the President's Advisory Council (P.A.C.), where I served for three years. I was the national president for the Professional Speakers Association of New Zealand. I successfully led cross-cultural teams across 15 international locations, and I am currently serving as the immediate past president of the Global Speakers Federation.

I was once $2,000,000 in debt and now I'm debt-free. I say all this not to impress you, but to impress upon you that if I can change, then so can you.

I can hear you moaning at me, "Not another self-help book! There's nothing new that Elias can tell me that I haven't heard before." The chances are that, like me, you have a stack of books on your bookshelf gathering dust, all promising you the elusive Holy Grail of leadership. People used to tell me that I wouldn't amount to much and that I was stupid, so the thought of improving myself was a remote fantasy. But I'm here to tell you that your past doesn't define your future. I want to encourage you to believe that you can change and start off with a clean sheet, using this book as the catalyst for your future self. Make this book your personal property, underlining passages that speak to you. Purchase a Bible and do the same with it. Use the margins to write your thoughts down. Buy a journal and keep a daily record of your thoughts. Your interactive participation in implementing the principles that I share in this book will dramatically improve your leadership capacity and retention of the material, both of which will impact your life, business and the key people who surround you.

I'm an executive coach, and I know the personal value that having a coach has had on my life. I'd like to coach you personally through your journey as you aspire to grow as a leader. Remember the last time you went on an aeroplane and sat through the safety briefing? What did the flight attendant tell you to do with the oxygen mask if it fell from the compartment above your head? Put it on the person sitting next to you? No – of course not! You were instructed to put it on yourself. Help yourself before you help those around you.

Are you ready to start leveraging God – giving you strength to help you achieve anything you desire? Now is the best time to start taking action. As I've said many times before, it's very hard to steer a parked car! Let's go!

LEVERAGING GOD

CHAPTER ONE

Are you making eye contact?

"Whatever you do, make sure you avoid making eye contact with her..."

This was the sage advice that my colleagues gave me in the Professional Speakers Association of New Zealand. It was late July 2013 and the Annual General Meeting was crouching around the corner, ready to pounce on the unsuspecting members, drawing them into service in a variety of roles.

Our President was looking to secure a committee to serve for the upcoming year. The roles of President, President-Elect and Speaker Coordinator were amongst many that she was looking to fill.

I already knew that I wanted to avoid any of the senior roles, so I was prepared when I got cornered during the networking time prior to our monthly meeting.

"Elias," she said, "Have you thought about serving as President for the Auckland Chapter?"

Our out-going President was hunting for her replacement and I felt the crosshairs focused on me.

I had previously worked on the committee under another President and the experience had tainted my view of volunteering to take on any senior role. My response was simple enough – I wasn't ready for that level of commitment. What I hadn't anticipated was her swift response.

"You should come in as President-Elect and serve for a year under David. This way you can gain experience from someone who can mentor you as we grow you into the role of President next year."

The thought of mentoring was appealing. I knew that I could learn. And what harm could come out of supporting David in the role? Without much thought, I agreed to be nominated for the role of President-Elect and signed the paperwork.

By the end of August, I was formally elected and looked forward to fulfilling this responsibility in the shadow of our Auckland Chapter President. Two weeks later I boarded a plane with my wife, Kay, and our two children, Brianna and Nicholas, as we headed over to New York City to start our five-week vacation.

What was supposed to be a relaxing time, attending my cousin's wedding on the East Coast and visiting my brother-in-law and his wife on our way to the West Coast (and the obligatory Disneyland treat for the kids), took a sublime twist...

One morning, whilst we were in Sedona, Arizona, I happened to be on-line checking my emails, when by chance one popped in from our new President, David. As I calculated the time zone difference, I realised that it was either the middle of the night back in New Zealand, or very early in the morning. I replied to his email and asked him if he was alright and if there was anything that I could do. His response was lukewarm.

I soon dismissed the thought of working and continued with our vacation. We were less than a week away from returning home.

After enjoying three days in Disneyland, we boarded our plane home. I turned my phone on to flight mode and settled into our 12-hour journey on board the Air New Zealand plane. Around 5am local time, our pilot woke us up with the announcement that we were going to be served breakfast as we started our

ARE YOU MAKING EYE CONTACT?

descent to Auckland International Airport.

I rubbed away the sleep from my eyes and selected the cooked breakfast. Monitoring the flight path on the screen in front of me, I counted down our arrival home. With clockwork precision, we landed on home soil in what proved to be an uneventful flight.

As we taxied to the gate, I turned my phone off flight mode. To my surprise, I saw the first inbound call come through. It had barely turned 7am and my colleagues from the Professional Speakers Association of New Zealand were calling me. I dismissed the call and sent the caller through to voicemail. Surely they knew that I had just returned after five weeks away. Whatever it was, it could wait!

To my surprize, they were quite persistent. I received a series of calls over the next couple of hours that I deliberately ignored. By 10am, I realised that no matter how often I ignored them, they seemed fixated on talking to me.

I eventually took a call whilst I was unpacking my luggage at home. Could I join them for a coffee? There was something that they needed to talk to me about in person. Resigned to the knowledge that if I didn't accept this kind offer, I would be fending off calls for the rest of the day, I noted the café that they wanted to meet in and, after showering and shaving, I left home half an hour later.

Over a coffee, they explained that David had to step down, for personal reasons, from the role of President for the Auckland Chapter. As President-Elect, I was asked whether I wanted to step up into the role vacated by David. And, suddenly, I became the Accidental President!

During my first National Board meeting, our National President announced that she was retiring from the Speaking industry. As a result, she would be stepping down as the New Zealand representative on the Global Speakers Federation Board. Would anybody like to take over? Without much thought, I put my hand up and asked her if I could find out more about the role.

The following week, she explained what the role entailed. But it took one well-positioned question to persuade me that I should take on the role.

"Do you want an international business?" she asked me.

I lived in Auckland, New Zealand. For me to be successful, everything that I did in my business needed to have an international focus. It was a no-brainer for me to accept the challenge. All I had to do was to attend as many international conferences, offer to serve and network with my colleagues. How difficult could that be?

When I asked what the next steps were, I was told that I needed to purchase my ticket to attend a conference, book a flight and pay for my hotel.

Where was it? Vancouver, Canada...

When was it? In six weeks' time...

So, six weeks and $6,000 later, I found myself in a fancy, 5-star hotel in Vancouver.

During the first day of the pre-conference, I attended a workshop. Halfway through the session, we had a toilet break. As I walked out of the room, I noticed a gentleman walk out of the adjoining room. We both searched for a gent's toilet on the second floor of this salubrious hotel but were thwarted in our attempt to find one.

Knowing that there was one on the ground floor, we both took the escalator down two flights to the ground floor. During this time, we struck up a conversation. The other gentleman introduced himself and the country that he came from. I told him that I was Elias, from New Zealand.

"New Zealand? I love the Māori!" he told me.

I shared my one and only Māori joke and he laughed!

As we returned to our respective workshops, we continued our conversation on the escalator.

"I'll be giving the closing Keynote at this conference," my new acquaintance told me. "Will you be coming to watch me?" Without hesitation, I told him that I was looking forward to it.

The next day I happened to exit the same room and guess what I saw directly in front of me? The entrance to the gent's toilet! It was as if God had put an invisibility cloak around the door to ensure that we couldn't see it and to force the two of us to have a conversation. Which got me thinking... "Why

ARE YOU MAKING EYE CONTACT?

didn't they find any weapons of mass destruction out in the Middle East?" Because they sent middle aged men to look for them!

You can imagine the scene. There is a middle-aged man standing beside his open fridge, looking perplexed and he calls out to his wife, "Honey, where's the butter?"

"It's there, right in front of you," she patiently replies!

Fast forward a couple of days, and we entered the final session of the conference. Eager to hear my new friend's closing Keynote speech, I squeezed into the main hall, alongside 407 hot and sweaty professional Speakers. As he got up on stage, can you guess what the first words were that came out of his mouth?

If you said, "Your Māori joke, Elias?" Nope!

The first words out of his mouth were: "Satan wants you to have a new name!"

The Speaker called himself a disruptor and he proceeded to spend the next 45 minutes glorifying Satan. He said many things that, as a man of faith, I found challenging to hear.

"Satan got sick and tired of being a prisoner of God in heaven that he came down to earth to get away from him!"

Now I had one of two choices. I could get up and walk out of the room like several of my Christian colleagues. Or I could choose to pray against his spirit. I chose option two.

He continued to glorify Satan and concluded his message by saying, "I prefer to spend eternity in hell, than one day as a prisoner of God in Heaven!"

Be careful what you ask for son, I thought, because that's exactly what you will get. As soon as the thought left my brain, I heard God speak. "Elias, it's time for you to take over the stage..."

I had no idea what that Word from God would mean. Some people would say that it was pre-destination and that He wanted me to head up the Global Speakers Federation (GSF). Others would argue that we are given free will, and, as a result, we could choose to go on a completely different path and avoid what God has planned for us.

Let's explore this. Imagine that you have a flowchart that gives you an option to choose which path you wanted to go. Maybe you can choose to say "YES" and go one way, or you can choose to say "NO" and go in the opposite direction. Does free will mean that if you choose "NO" that you will end up somewhere that you were not supposed to be?

I have a theory that I'd like to explore with you. This theory is called "The Loophole Theory".

You know that when we create laws, invariably there is a loophole in that law. Which is why, I guess, that so many criminals seem to get away with their crime, due to these loopholes that appear. What if God has a "Loophole Theory" in His laws? How would that affect us when He's already given us free will?

You may have heard the story of Jonah, where he is swallowed by a big fish and ends up spending three days in its stomach. For me, the story is one of free will and loopholes.

God reaches out to Jonah and asks him to go to Nineveh, where He wants Jonah to preach to them so that they can be saved. Jonah, who has free will, arrives at the port in Joppa and there he invokes his free will and chooses to take another ship that is heading in the opposite direction. He buys his ticket to Tarshish. At this point, you could be excused for thinking that this is the end of the story.

However, God has a plan and He will invoke one of His loopholes to ensure that it is fulfilled.

As the ship was on its way, God sends a mighty wind and the boat is lurching in the tempestuous seas, about to break. The sailors were afraid and started to throw cargo overboard, in the hope of saving themselves and the boat. Unsuccessful in their attempts, one of the sailors remembers that Jonah is asleep in the bowels of the ship.

When they awake him from his slumber, they ask him if he has any idea why the storm has hit them. "Funny that you should ask," Jonah replies. "I think that I do!" With that, he offers to be thrown from the ship, which they eventually do, and this is followed by the calm as the sailors and ship are saved from destruction.

The story could easily, once again, have stopped at this point. But it doesn't. Jonah is bobbing in the water, left to take his chances, when a big fish enters, stage right, and proceeds to swallow Johan up. For three days Jonah was in the belly of the big fish, which eventually arrives at the shoreline off Nineveh. On cue, the fish vomits Jonah up and he is delivered to the place that God had pre-destined for him.

Free will vs predestination.

What if Jonah had chosen to take a ship to Nineveh when he was at Joppa. Maybe he would have arrived at his destination, had one look around him and said, "You know what? I don't like the Ninevites. Never have, never will! I ain't gonna do what God has asked me to do."

Trust me, God would have had another plan to persuade Jonah to carry on. After all, he has used a talking donkey to do His work in the past (you can read about this in the Bible in Numbers 22:21-39).

What we find out is that Jonah walked the length of Nineveh, preaching to them over the course of three days, and everyone got saved!

I encourage you to read the book of Jonah in the Bible. What is fascinating to me is that the book is only 4 chapters long, yet three-and-a-half of these chapters deals with Jonah's rebellion against God's instruction. John Maxwell, in The Maxwell Leadership Bible makes the following commentary: *"It is interesting to note that every major player in the story – the storm, the sailors, the fish, the king, The Ninevites, the vine, the worm and the east wind – all obey God ... except for Jonah, the leader God chose."*

Maxwell goes on to explain that *"despite Jonah's disobedience, his lack of perspective, his cultural prejudice, his self-righteousness, his wrong motives, and his bad attitude, God never gave up on him."*

Like Jonah, I could have used free will to walk away from the conference and the word that God had given me. Or it could just be predestination that God would eventually get me to where He wanted me to be...

TIME TO REFLECT...

What are some of the learning lessons in this experience?

We have free will and we can exercise it the way that we want to.

If the choice that you make is contrary to God's choice, it doesn't mean that you will have to suffer bad things going forward.

If God wants you do something or be somewhere, He will find a loophole to get you there!

LEVERAGING GOD

CHAPTER TWO

What is your secret name?

My good friend and fellow Founding Partner of the John Maxwell Team, Kary Oberbrunner, wrote a fascinating book entitled, "Your Secret Name". A Pastor at Grace Church in Ohio, Kary drew me to him through the words that he crafted in his book.

"What's your name?"

We hear that question almost every day. Yet many of us don't know who we really are. We spend so much time trying to meet the expectations of others and overcome the pressures we put on ourselves that we forget how much more God has in store for us.

As the back cover of Kary's book explains, the biblical patriarch Jacob spent years living out the meaning of his earthly name – deceiver. Only when he stopped accepting the names the world pinned on him did he hear God speak his true name. Only then could he understand the vision God had for his life.

Using Jacob's story as a powerful backdrop, Kary calls us to abandon what we know so we can become who we were born to be. Jacob was unaware that God would build a nation through him. He was unaware that Jesus, the promised Redeemer, would be one of his descendants. He was unaware of the lands he would one day inherit. Until he heard his Heavenly Father whisper his Secret Name.

You might be unaware of God's plans for you. You might not be able to fathom what God wants to build through you. You can hardly imagine the lands He wants you to inherit. Until you truly wrestle with God, until you hear God whisper Your Secret Name.

Are you ready to listen?

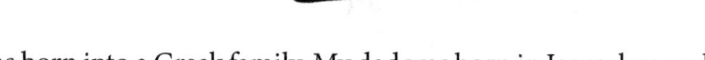

I was born into a Greek family. My dad was born in Jerusalem and my mother in Bethlehem. Both Greek Orthodox Christians, I remember growing up in a Christian household, with the Church being the center of our world.

My mother used to tell me that we were from the same tribe as Jesus. No pressure!!

Born in Tripoli, Libya, the youngest of three siblings, I can say that life was idyllic.

Social interaction was a picnic at the beach where face-time was the norm and Facebook was yet to be invented! Everyone I knew was 'adopted' as part of my extended family and they were lovingly referred to as 'Aunty' or 'Uncle'. In fact, two of these lovely ladies - Aunty Souad and Aunty Fairuz - would one day be referred to as two surrogate mothers at my first wedding in London!

We lived in a multi-cultural society. I was surrounded by Italians, British, Americans, and the whole Arab League. Our social network was centered around the Greek Orthodox Church. It was safe to say that I had a good life, and there were good memories.

My mother was a teacher. She was a beautiful woman, Hollywood-esque in her black and white wedding photo.

My father came to Libya via Jordan because of his banking career. He brought a great deal of banking experience, but he also imported much more.

A full-blooded Greek, as the head of the household, he demanded respect within his own home. Despite his outward appearance, he was and continued to be, a loving father. He just didn't know how to command respect through cooperation and connection. Therefore, he reverted to the only way that he knew - brute force and domination.

This translated to a barking command, which occasionally escalated into physical assertion, delivered via his leather belt. The recipients were my brother and sister. It seems that I was spared his wrath - and I believe I had my mother to thank for this.

But was this blessing actually a hindrance in disguise?

I may have been spared my father's physical wrath, but because of his inability to connect at a deeper level, my father reverted to another form of control over me – verbal.

One of my father's favorite words was 'idiot'. Everyone was an idiot.

The person at the dairy was an idiot; the attendant at the petrol station was an idiot; and – yes you guessed it – even I was an idiot!

Growing up in an upper middle-class family, I never wanted for anything. I had a roof over my head, food in my stomach and clothes on my back. I even went on to attend private schools in the UK and some would suggest that I was bordering on the elite. My family wasn't outwardly dysfunctional, and I never questioned my upbringing. Instead, I enjoyed what I took to be an idyllic lifestyle. Yet, I had no idea of the impact these words were having on me. I would discover later that the constant reinforcement of this message had a devastating effect on me.

As the youngest child, I was spared the belt and other forms of physical punishment that I saw my siblings endure. My punishment, it turns out, whilst predominantly mental, had much deeper and longer-lasting scars than anything physical that I might have observed.

The punishment didn't stop with my father and his domineering personality. It was subconsciously fed by my mother's caustic comments about my father. This statement warrants an explanation...

The best way to describe my father was to call him a chauvinist. In fact, it probably wouldn't be surprising if most Greek men of his generation were anything but chauvinistic in their outlook and actions. He did what he was taught by his father who in turn was taught by his father. They believed this to be the right way to treat women and children.

Most children will pick the signs of dysfunction in a household. They don't have to see it; they can sense it. I instinctively knew when my parents were arguing because of their raised voices that I often heard from my bedroom. But I would notice it more in my mother's bloodshot and teary eyes.

Why make such an inflammatory statement as this? Because I was told that, at the age of five, I approached my mother and told her that I wanted to get a knife and use it to stab my father in the back because of the things that he did to her...

The funny thing is that I had no direct recollection of this fact. And yet, it has been presented to me on many occasions as a "fait accompli"!

The messenger, as it happens, was my mother.

On numerous occasions, from an early age through to my mid-40's, my mother would repeat this story in casual conversation to me and occasionally with any others who might be listening.

Was this a true statement and a reflection of the actual turn of events when I was five years old? The reality is I had no idea. The sad truth is, fact or fiction, this constant reinforcement had devastating consequences. It resulted in a potentially planted memory, which led to a distorted view that I carried about my father.

Intentional or not, it contributed to a growing resentment that I harbored for my father which undoubtedly created anger and separation between us. I didn't like my father when I was growing up and I always wanted to side with my mother whenever possible. If questioned, I'm sure that my father would have called me "stubborn" in connection to our relationship.

Either way, the damage had been done from a very early age. To an impressionable young lad, every word that my father pointed in my direction was barbed with hate and manipulated into a reinforcement of my father's contempt for me and my idiotic nature.

According to Kary Oberbrunner, we have a total of three names:

1) **Birth Name** – the name assigned to you when you arrived in this world.
2) **Given Name** – the names you inherit walking in this world (positive and negative).
3) **Secret Name** – the name granted to you by the One who made you.

When you look at these individually, it is easy to see that these names are given to us by others.

Our parents can sometimes labor for ages to select our birth names. I remember agonizing for months over the name of our son. Kay considered the name Nicholas, which I simply refused to accept. I toyed with the name Cameron. I even went as far as creating an email address using that name and sent her emails from our unborn son. Suddenly, less than two months before he was born, I changed my mind and decided that Nicholas should be his name. Either way, I know that Nicholas had no say in what his name was when he was born!

We get Birth Names that sometimes are passed from generation to generation. Others receive the trendy name that accompanies a royal child. Irrespective of the lineage, these names are often recorded on birth certificates and allocated to the child.

But, as we grow up, we seem to inherit a second name – our Given Name.

These names tend to be similar to nick-names. They get handed to us in the schoolyard by other kids (some well-meaning and some just mean). Maybe through a teacher. Or a parent.

Four-eyes.

Fat.

Loser.

Adopted.

Idiot.

I'm sure that if you took the time to think about it, you can identify a number of names that were given to you. Names that tended to define your identity as you were growing up. Names that hurt you as you grew up. Names that stained your soul.

Your name could be a positive name.

Beautiful.

Athlete.

These names can also define your identity. But what happens if you are 'Beautiful' and lose your looks in a fire and your face becomes disfigured? What happens to your identity?

Or if you are an Athlete, and you break your leg and terminate your career. What happens to your identity then?

What if these Given Names were a lie? What if we have bought into that lie that "Satan wants you to have a new name?" In the Bible, Jesus refers to Satan as the "father of all lies" in John 8:44. Satan is described as a murderer, who does not stand in truth, because there is no truth in him.

Are you falling for this lie, trapped in the identity of your Given Name?

But what if we didn't have to live this Groundhog Day of lies forever...

The Bible also reveals that there is more to us and about us. In the book of Revelation, it states:

> "To him who overcomes... I will give him a white stone and on the stone a new name written which no one knows except him who receives it." (Revelation 2:17, NKJV)

We all have one – a Secret Name that is. Yet few of us know ours. Ignorantly, we're stuck, caught up in the "Name Game," searching for our true identity. It's time to go deep, past clichés to discover Your Secret Name and the vision God has for your life.

I received my Secret Name whilst MCing a Your Secret Name event for Kary in Columbus Ohio back in 2013. It was life-changing.

As a boy who grew up with the Given Name of 'Idiot', my academic career bore witness to my name. I was the dunce in my class, coming rock bottom throughout my scholastic years. This extended to my undergraduate years and crept into my career.

Having scraped through my degree living under the misconception that I was the village idiot, my grades reinforced what I had been told about myself.

What chance did I have to succeed? I certainly didn't deserve to get any better.

This continual self-inflicted injury was reinforced by years of self-doubt. I bought into the lie of the enemy at an early age. That lie affected my relationships and my career. I would secure a job, lasting between 12 and 30 months in the position, before I had to move on. I thought that I couldn't hold on to a role. What I didn't realize was that no role could outgrow me.

As I asked in my book, "Liberating Your Leadership Potential" – How old do you have to be to become a leader?

Irrespective of your age, I want to encourage you to understand that leadership has nothing to do with the mechanics of a chronometer.

Upon graduating from university with my Master of Science degree in 1984, I joined the workforce in a full-time capacity. Aged twenty-two, I started my role as Electronic Test Engineer. It wasn't a glamorous role, but it provided me with an acceptable income that helped me to pay for my first car.

The timing of my appointment coincided with the promotion of my manager from Head of Electronic Test to Operations Manager. I was told to hang tight and to report to him until a replacement was found. As it turned out, over the next six weeks, candidates rode a merry-go-round through the office door – unable to secure the role. When I was approached about taking over as Head of Department, I was chuffed (that's English for honored!). If the truth be told, I was quite cocky about being selected. But this turned out to be a baptism of fire.

It certainly proved that age wasn't a barrier to leadership roles, but my lack of leadership experience was compensated for by strong interpersonal skills.

Some of the readers will see the writing on the wall and recognize that there wasn't any coincidence between the timing of the promotion and my leadership capabilities. Did this fit in with the 'Idiot' Given Name that I had adopted?

Yet the ingrained identity created by this name I had received totally blinded me to the possibilities that I was made for bigger and better things. I thought that I needed to move on because I was self-sabotaging in my career. I felt that I had reached my limit in each role and needed to escape before I was found out as a fraud.

What hindsight has given me is the ability to understand that I had outgrown the role and I was looking for another challenge to stimulate my brain and allow me to continue to grow. It turns out that I was no dummy after all.

My children will tell you that I love the phrase, "You're either green and growing or ripe and rotting!" I'm 58 years old at the time of writing this book and I can tell you that I have a lot more in me that needs to come out! I'm definitely not ripe and rotting yet. So how could I have seen myself as rotting at the tender age of my early 20's?

Where are you in your journey of life? Have you surrendered to a life of mediocrity? Do you believe in the lies of your Given Name?

What if, this side of eternity, you could break through and find Your Secret Name?

Can I encourage you to go to Kary's website, YourSecretName.com and take the quiz there to help you find yours? What do you have to lose?

So, in case you were wondering what my Secret Name was, here it is – Wonderful!

TIME TO REFLECT...

What are some of the learning lessons in this experience?

I had lived a lie by accepting my Given Name of 'idiot'.

The enemy will try to distract you and create self-doubt about you and your true identity.

You can receive your Secret Name this side of eternity.

Whatever has happened in your life to date, please hold on to the idea that things can change and that there is more in store for you. All you have to do is to understand that God loves you and wants the best for you.

LEVERAGING GOD

CHAPTER THREE

Why did Eve's bite affect me?

Imagine if one day, à la 'The Truman Show', you woke up to find that everything you believed was the result of careful manipulation of your life by someone else? What if much of what you believed was a lie? Well, for you, that day has arrived...

2007 was a watershed year for me. It marked a financial breakthrough. With God's help, I managed to clear $160,000 of debt in less than six months. This followed a revelation that my wife and I had when we were water baptized. As we arose from the waters, cleaned and new, God said to us, "In two years' time you will be debt-free." That day was the 8th of May 2005.

Later in this book, I will explain in detail what God did to get us debt-free.

When His word came to fruition, I found myself working in the corporate world. I had been head-hunted into a role that gave me a 25% pay increase. Thanks to His timing, I also qualified for five-figure bonus payments from my previous employer. You will get to understand the power of God when you read that these bonuses were authorized ON the day that I left. Logic would indicate that I would not qualify for them, but logic has nothing to do with His will...

Debt-free, and cruising in my job, I found myself reading a fascinating book called "Eve's Bite" by investigative journalist and author, Ian Wishart. The description of his book reads as follows:

> "In an age dominated by 'spin', you are about to discover that the best spin campaigns of all are the ones you never even knew about. In the most politically-incorrect book ever published in this country, journalist Ian Wishart rounds up a herd of sacred cows – demolishing Richard Dawkins, sideswiping the anti-smacking lobbyists, skewering the social engineers and exposing the elites who want your taxes and your children while they laugh all the way to the bank like perverse Pied Pipers."

This book is an in-depth analysis of the way that the political propaganda machines work. Drawing a parallel to the Nazi party, modern-day political parties and their messaging systems are analyzed and dissected.

If you've ever read the book '1984' by George Orwell, you probably have images of the mind police and big brother monitoring your every move. Manipulation of history is made up of using "Newspeak" a controlled language of restricted grammar and limited vocabulary, meant to limit the freedom of thought — personal identity, self-expression, free will.

Wishart paints a bleak picture. Supported by documented evidence, he shows how the same methodologies that the Nazis employed in the lead up to World War II are still being used by modern-day political parties. I love the way that his book is summarised in the blog by John Dierckx, entitled "The Desk of the Renaissance Man" where he says:

> "Wishart is not afraid in the choice of his subjects: Karl Marx, Nazi propaganda techniques, Charles Darwin & intelligent design, Richard Dawkins, the gay rights movement, the "safe sex" campaign, abortion and trade in body parts, the anti-smacking campaign, liberal education, the mainstream media eugenics and, Islam and the threat to the west. He managed to bring them all together and identifies the relationships between them in a more than just compelling way. Having enjoyed

a rather liberal approach to life and society this book was most certainly an eye-opener that made me rethink certain positions."
(ref: https://johndierckx.wordpress.com/2007/05/16/boom-review-ian-wishart-eves-bite/)

An eye-opener indeed!

When I tell people about this book, I ask whether they have a strong stomach. You will certainly need it when you get to understand how much you – and more importantly your children – have been lied to.

I felt as if I had been the frog that is left in a cauldron of water that is sitting on a fire. As the temperature rises, the frog just sits there enjoying the warming waters, unaware that it is slowly being boiled to death. Reading Eve's bite made me consciously aware that I was being killed by my surroundings. I no longer wanted to become a negligent bystander allowing the government to lie to me.

One of the main reasons I chose New Zealand as my home back in 1995 related to the place where I believed my children would grow up in a safe and protected environment.

You may remember reading about the horrific abduction, torture and subsequent murder of a two-year-old boy called James Bulger in Liverpool during February 1993. What made this event significantly abhorrent was that the perpetrators of the crime were two ten-year-old boys.

At the time of the crime, my eldest daughter was nearly three years old and my ex-wife was pregnant with my second daughter. We were looking at emigrating to Australia, where my ex-wife was born. Alternative destinations included the USA (where my family were based) and Italy (where my employer was headquartered). One day, an acquaintance suggested that I should consider New Zealand.

Not knowing about the country, my research was accidentally started when I came across an episode of the late Clive James' show "Clive James On Television".

An Australian journalist and satirist, James irreverently mocked television from around the world. Like millions, I watched this every Sunday evening mainly to laugh at the clips of horrible foreign programs such as 'Endurance', 'Ultra Quiz' and 'The Price Is Right'. Back in the early '80s, we thought that we could safely laugh in the knowledge that our television was the best in the world.

One particular episode that I watched included TV from New Zealand. James unveiled a scene from 'Crimewatch New Zealand' with the usual aplomb associated with an Aussie's contempt of his fellow cousins from 'across the ditch'. The clip was presented by a police officer and his female colleague introducing themselves, asking the audience for their help to solve the following crime: someone had their shopping stolen from their Holden car, outside of the supermarket in the suburb of Remuera. Now, I thought, if this is the crime, then this is the country for me!

TIME TO REFLECT...

What are some of the learning lessons in this experience?

The propaganda machine is alive and kicking. We are being lied to on a daily basis.

We are like the frog that is sitting in a cauldron full of water, unaware that underneath the cauldron is a lit fire, slowly warming up the water. As the temperature rises, the frog sits contented, enjoying the warming water that surrounds it. Unfortunately, this water reaches boiling point, by which time it is too late for the frog to escape.

The media has been manipulating our worldview and has the ability to shift popular thought.

CHAPTER FOUR

Why is New Zealand the land of the Long White Underbelly?

Little did I know that by moving halfway across the world to Aotearoa, the land of the long white cloud, that I would, in fact, be bringing my family over to something that was even more septic.

Wishart, in his book, opened my eyes to the fact that I, alongside most of my compatriots, were becoming blind and apathetic to the brainwashing that was our daily bread.

There is a common phrase that you often hear that goes like this: "She'll be right". NO!! She'll not be right; something is terribly wrong. I found myself living in a country that was manipulating my view of what life should look like.

The government of the day was developing polices on snacks in the Ministry of Health snack machines. People were telling me what kind of "brain snack" my daughter requires at school. Worst of all, laws like the anti-smacking bill were being passed despite an abundance of public resistance.

This was during a term of nine-years of left-wing political dominance of the Labour Party, headed by the immensely talented Helen Clarke. Despite politicians being implicated in all kinds of alleged corruption, the government of the day continued with its disinformation campaigns like "no hubba without a rubba".

Under the Fair Trading Act, I would be found liable if I provide false information about products or services I sell. Yet the government was trying to sell me on the use of condoms to protect me and the younger generations against sexually transmitted diseases against which condoms are not known to protect! How thick can you be and still breathe? You had to wonder if the policymakers were reading comics as they came to this conclusion.

After reading this book, I started a conversation with Paul Adams. Paul was originally a carpenter and joiner before he established a business manufacturing outdoor playground equipment. Soon after, he became a professional rally driver and won three prestigious New Zealand championships.

Paul also became a politician, entering New Zealand parliament as a list candidate for the United Future party in 2002. Our paths crossed in 2005 when Kay and I started fellowshipping at City Impact Church, a Pentecostal Church on the North Shore of Auckland. Paul ventured out as an independent candidate and contested the 2005 general election in the East Coast Bays electorate. I got involved in his local campaign, delivering candidate leaflets and door-knocking on his behalf in the lead up to the election.

Paul gained 5,809 votes after a short five-week campaign, which placed him third overall.

I maintained a casual interest in his political ambitions whilst I got to know him and his family through our involvement at Church. It was only after I read Wishart's book that I plucked up the courage to ask Paul what his plans were for the upcoming election scheduled for 2008.

He said that he was looking to co-found a new Christian political party. Little did I know that this would lead me away from my corporate role and into the political field that I was unqualified for. Paul introduced me to an ex-police officer by the name of Richard 'Richie' Lewis. It was during this time that the Family Party was founded. I was invited to join the diverse Board, which I accepted.

Paul then became the Deputy Leader of The Family Party. Richie was the Leader.

As a Board, we would meet once a week, setting policy, selecting candidates and working through the logistics of the political landscape that we had to traverse.

Nearly four months into this new adventure, Kay and I spoke about starting a three-week fast. We were independently seeking a word from God in relation to the pathways that He had planned for us.

If you are unfamiliar with the concept of fasting, the best description that I have come across was given by Pastor Rick Warren, who describes fasting as "a spiritual discipline that is taught in the Bible. Jesus expected His followers to fast, and He said that God rewards fasting. Fasting, according to the Bible, means to voluntarily reduce or eliminate your intake of food for a specific time and purpose."

> [16] "When you fast [give up eating], don't put on a sad face like the hypocrites. They make their faces look sad to show people they are fasting [giving up eating]. [17] I tell you the truth, those hypocrites already have their full reward. So when you fast [give up eating], comb your hair and wash your face. Then people will not know that you are fasting [giving up eating], but your Father, whom you cannot see, will see you. Your Father sees what is done in secret, and he will reward you."
> (Matthew 6:16-18, NCV)

After our discussion, both Kay and I were in agreement about what we were seeking God's confirmation for. Kay was seeking God's guidance in relation to her studies and I was seeking His guidance in relation to volunteering my time for the next year with the Family Party.

Our fast started on a Monday morning. On Tuesday evening, as I was completing my second day without food, I attended a Family Party Board meeting. During the evening, I spoke with Paul and said that I was thinking about dedicating a year without pay to the Family Party. His response, along the lines of "That's nice!" was totally underwhelming.

When I spoke to Richie, I expected a more positive outcome to my announcement. Needless to say, my high expectations were not met!

The following day, Richie and Paul met up in the Family Party headquarters in Mangere, South Auckland. There they commented to each other that I had approached them to offer my services to the Family Party. Wondering how genuine I was about this, they decided to call me.

As I took the call from Paul, he asked, "Were you serious about what you said to me last night?"

After I confirmed that I was, he told me that he and Richie had an idea that they wanted to run past me. Was I available to meet up with them the following day to discuss this? We set a time to meet up on the Thursday. I thought that they were going to ask me to become Paul's campaign manager and help him run the campaign on the North Shore. I went to sleep contented, if somewhat hungry, that night.

I met up with Richie and Paul the following day and, over a cup of coffee, they again quizzed me about my desire to volunteer my time for the Family Party. My response was unequivocal. I was committed – 100%! I was willing to do ANYTHING that they asked.

They then prayed for me before they shared their plan. Once again, they asked if I had any idea what role I would like to take on. I reiterated that I had total faith in them and their judgment. Whatever they suggested, I would do.

Then Richie told me, "Elias, we would like you to become the Party President!"

You could have knocked me over with a feather. I was blindsided. Not even I saw this coming!

I had no political experience, let alone political aspirations, yet I found myself holding one of the most powerful positions within that party at the time. Richie and Paul saw something in me that I didn't see in myself.

As I mentioned earlier, I accepted their judgment. They were the leaders and I was to follow them. Without hesitation, I accepted the role.

On my drive back to the office, where I was going to hand in my notice, I called Kay to tell her the outcome of our meeting. My call went through to voicemail, where I announced that I was about to give my notice and start my new calling. We were already debt-free, and it made sense for me to make a clean break. I finished the message by asking a question. "Now that God has answered my prayer, can I stop fasting?"

When I got into the office, I wrote out my letter of resignation and handed it to my boss. In four short weeks, I would exit the corporate world for the last time.

Oh, in case you were wondering, Kay answered my question by the time she returned home that evening. All she said was, "A fast is a fast. Three weeks means three weeks – you can keep going!"

TIME TO REFLECT...

What are some of the learning lessons in this experience?

If there was one thing that I could counsel you to do, it would be this – consult with your spouse before you make a life-changing decision. Where there is unity, it commands a blessing. The psalmist wrote about this, Psalm 133:

> *"¹How good and pleasant it is*
> *when God's people live together in unity!*
> *²It is like precious oil poured on the head,*
> *running down on the beard,*
> *running down on Aaron's beard,*
> *down on the collar of his robe.*
> *³It is as if the dew of Hermon*
> *were falling on Mount Zion.*
> *For there the Lord bestows his blessing,*
> *even life forevermore."*
> (Psalm 133:1-3, NIV)

The campaign that we waged during that election was based on a unified vision and purpose. I encourage you to seek out God's word in relation to unity. Here are a couple of bible verses that you can search out and meditate on:

1 Corinthians 1:10
Romans 12:16
Acts 4:32
Philippians 1:27
Genesis 2:24

LEVERAGING GOD

CHAPTER FIVE

What does it take to go from Zero to Hero?

What needs to happen to propel an Idiot into a President? To answer this, I'd like to take you on a journey through time that starts off in my childhood and ends with my salvation...

As you may have already gathered, my early life did not groom me for the position of President for the Family Party. My life trajectory was one of mediocrity, at best. But what happened that altered that course?

With parents born in the Holy Land and an alleged lineage that can be traced straight back to Jesus, I knew, from an early age, that God was real and that Jesus was my savior.

> "God so loved the world that he sent his one and only Son, that whoever believes in him shall not perish but have eternal life."
> (John 3:16, NIV)

I believed that Jesus came to earth and was made flesh. That He died for our sins in a cruel and painful way on the cross in Calvary.

I remember going to Church every Sunday and attending Sunday school. All the normal things that a kid born in the 60s would do. By the time we left Libya in 1970 and started living in London, nothing had materially changed. We still attended the Greek Orthodox Church every week and I started attending a group called The Crusaders in the afternoon.

It was a Christian youth program run by the Christian Union. This became a regular Sunday afternoon activity for me that I eagerly anticipated each week. I would read through my Bible and answer as many questions as possible to gain the points required to read a scripture or qualify for a prize.

During summer, I attended a camping trip with this group and found myself enjoying the outdoors. Even Kay would tell you that I'm not known as a camper. (My idea of 'roughing it' is waiting an hour for room service!) This would prove to be the only time in my recollection that I tackled the great outdoors.

I was confident with my Bible stories and each time I surrounded myself with this group, it provided me with a sense of release from my father's negative and insulting remarks. What I learned there was that there was a living, loving God that cared for each and every one of us. Not the dark and rigid God that I was brought up to believe that He was.

At the tender age of eleven, I started attending boarding school. I was the youngest in my class as well as my year. This gave me a reprise from my father as I was only able to see him during the school holidays. Whilst my brother was also in the same boarding house as me, it didn't necessarily give me any privileges. But it did force me to become independent.

The boarding school experience didn't seem to diminish my love for God or my involvement with the Crusaders. We would regularly attend chapel services and each Sunday I would participate in the Sunday service. The main difference was that we swapped the Greek liturgy for a free-flowing, shorter, English-based service that I could better understand!

By the age of fifteen, I remember joining a small group of fellow students and participating in a weekly Bible study program. We would meet in the study of one of the older boys and select some scripture and review it amongst ourselves.

On one occasion, I remember that we completed our Bible study when the senior boy announced that we were going to close in prayer. At this point, I lowered my head in reverence and respect and expected the others to join me in this action. Much to my horror, the boy leading us proceeded to lift his head and arms up to the ceiling and started to thank God and pray.

This was a step too far for me. I looked up and challenged him. I asked him what he thought he was doing and he simply said, "Praying."

I was not having a bar of what this boy was saying. Through the lens of the Greek Orthodox Church, I perceived that he was disrespecting God through his actions. In fact, I went one stage further and accused the boy of being a Pharisee – a clean cup on the outside, but dirty on the inside.

Needless to say, the boy wasn't impressed. He asked me to apologize and I simply refused. He went on to report me to my headmaster, who also took the side of this boy. Again, I was asked to apologize. Once more, I refused. With one final attempt to reconcile this situation, my housemaster tried to find a middle ground, which I stubbornly refused to shift on to. The consequence of maintaining this stance, I was told, was that I would receive six lashes of the cane.

You have to understand that I was always a goody-two-shoes as a kid growing up. I NEVER got into trouble and yet here I found myself fast approaching my first hiding. I had seen my brother and sister receive the belt from my father, but I never imagined that this would happen to me.

I prepared myself for the fate that awaited and duly received my six lashes. I left the headmasters' office with tears welling up in my eyes.

I was angry. It was at that point that I made a decision to walk away from God and to take my own path.

It took me 30 years of walking in the wilderness before I finally returned to a relationship with God, inviting Jesus into my heart. Thirty fruitless, painful and unfulfilling years.

Why did I walk away? That's a great question. It took me a long time until I finally figured it out.

In the northern hemisphere summer of 2013, when I was in the USA attending the Your Secret Name conference, I went out with my colleague and YSN Coach, Desiree, for an ice cream. As we selected our exotically named ice creams, I shared the story of calling the boy a Pharisee and subsequently walking away from God.

To this point in time, now nearly 40 years on from the event, I hadn't really analyzed the rationale behind my decision to walk away from God. Desiree looked at me, her spoon full of ice cream hovering in mid-air between her bowl and her mouth. Pausing in-between mouthfuls of ice cream, she pointed her spoon back at me and asked the question, "Do you know why you walked away from God?"

Honestly, no I didn't. As I mentioned, I hadn't given it much thought.

With the insight given to her by the Holy Spirit, her words cut like a sword through bone and marrow as she gave me the explanation. "Elias," she said, "you were angry with God. You tried to defend Him at that point, and you perceived that He had let you down!"

Desiree's explanation made perfect sense. It was something that I was blinded to for ages. It was yet another lie from the enemy that I had swallowed, hook, line, and sinker! I felt so foolish and realized that I had wasted so much potential over such a long period of my life.

My wife likes to remind me that nothing is wasted in God. I may have been in the wilderness for 30 years, but at least I had evolved compared to the tribe of Israel who had spent 40 years wandering in the wilderness before they found the promised land.

Despite my isolation from God, I still believed in Him. I knew the parables that Jesus shared and the stories from the Old Testament. Everything that I had absorbed in Sunday School and through The Crusaders had embedded itself in my heart.

Having made the decision to walk away from God, people have asked me why

I eventually returned to Him. To understand this I want to take you back to 1998, when I had the opportunity to establish my own Amway business. My upline Diamonds were a Christian couple called Simon and Yvonne Godfrey. One of the first business events that I attended was a five-hour seminar that was hosted at a location called Bay Christian Fellowship. The guest speaker was from the USA. He delivered four hour-long Keynotes that were titled "The Ethics of Business". As I listened to him speak, I recognized each story. He sourced them from the Bible!

He put a modern-day spin on the story and made it relevant to the 21st-century business audience that he was preaching to. I say "preaching" because, yes, you guessed it, the guest speaker was a Pastor from the USA.

At the end of this seminar, we were told that he would be preaching at a Church in Newmarket the following day. I looked at Kay and encouraged her to attend this service.

The next morning, we traveled to Newmarket and attended the small Church service. For me, this was nothing new. Yet for Kay, this was virgin territory. Her father was not vocal about his belief in a God, and might have been referred to as a new-ager. As for Kay, she had never stepped into a Church outside of weddings and funerals.

I can't remember what the sermon was about that Sunday morning. All I know was that at the end of the service we were all invited to bow our heads and close our eyes. The Pastor was taking an altar call.

Both Kay and I responded, and we came up to the front of the Church and repeated a short prayer that invited Jesus into our hearts. We filled in a form and passed over our contact details. That was the last time that we saw or heard from anybody at that Church.

Have you heard the phrase, "Nothing changes, but everything has changed"?

I expected that we would receive a call at the very least from a member of that congregation, but to my surprise, nothing further transpired.

Kay and I continued our heathen lifestyles and got married in December 1998. By 2001 we welcomed our daughter Brianna to this world. Within 15 months, her brother Nicholas would come to complete our family.

Our Amway business was growing steadily but never exploded to its full potential. My career was also steadily projecting in an upward pathway. We found some level of success, but deep down there was something missing from our life.

Just before Christmas, 2004, Simon and Yvonne invited us to a private counseling session at their house on the North Shore. We were given one task in preparation for our meeting. Kay and I were to independently write our goals – short-term (next 12 months), medium-term (1-5 years) and long-term (5-10 years) – and prioritize them from the most important to least.

At the juncture during dinner between the main course and dessert, Simon asked us who was willing to share their goals. Being the shy and retiring type, I offered to go first!

The top priority on my short-term goals I had written: 'To be planted in a good Church'.

I knew that I knew that I knew that if I didn't get my life and relationship aligned with God, nothing that I put my efforts into would lead to any recognizable form of success. As Kay said, there was a God-shaped hole in our hearts that nothing else could fill.

Yvonne didn't need another opportunity. She invited us to attend Church and we set up a time in January 2005 to come to a night service at a Church called City Impact Church.

When we arrived on that Sunday night and drove up into the carpark, there was something strangely familiar in this building. I would later be told that this Church used to be called Bays Christian Fellowship and happened to be the same location where the Pastor had presented the four business lectures to us in 1998.

By this stage, I was a little wary of what was going to happen. I had heard that this was a Pentecostal Church, so I expected to hear loud music. And I wasn't disappointed.

With my arms crossed, I attempted to repel the music and was determined not to be influenced by it. Despite my best efforts, I noticed that my feet were tapping along to the rhythm of the drumbeat. Eventually, I uncrossed my arms and let myself be drawn into the songs, warbling along as best as I could to the lyrics on the screen.

This unconventional service continued with a young Pastor coming on to the stage and sharing a message with the congregation. Throughout his message, I remember nodding my head and agreeing with what he said.

By the end of his sermon, we were all asked to bow our heads and close our eyes. I knew what was coming next...

I obliged by bowing my head but managed to peek out of my right eye to see what Kay would do when the call would eventually be made to ask Jesus into our hearts. (I knew that I wanted to do this, but I wasn't going to do this alone!)

As the altar-call came, I strained my right eye to see what Kay was doing. Maybe I was willing her on, I can't tell, but I was relieved to see her hand go up.

"I see that hand," the Pastor announced. That was my cue to raise my hand. "I see that hand," he went on to say.

We were two of four salvations from that service.

After the service, we joined Simon and Yvonne for a coffee. Simon led us through the bookstore where he helped me to pick out a bible. Without hesitation, he showed me The Maxwell Leadership Bible, which I immediately added to my book collection.

TIME TO REFLECT...

What are some of the learning lessons in this experience?

God is always waiting for you. He has chosen you before you were formed in your mother's womb.

> *"I knew you before I formed you in your mother's womb. Before you were born I set you apart and appointed you as my prophet to the nations."*
> (Jeremiah 1:5, NLT)

If I thought about all of the sins that I had committed when I was wandering in the wilderness, I would have enough material to fill many volumes that cover my exploits. Any judge who saw my misdemeanours would throw the book at me. Luckily, God has an alternative plan. He is willing to forgive and forget.

> *"But I, yes I, am the one*
> *who takes care of your sins—that's what I do.*
> *I don't keep a list of your sins."*
> (Isaiah 43:25, MSG)

CHAPTER SIX

Why is it relevant to connect to John Maxwell and the 21 Irrefutable Laws of Leadership?

If you can remember this principle, then you will realise that there is a chance for you to turn things around.

When I first came to New Zealand, I quickly found myself in a position where I was earning a great six-figure salary. I was tasked to develop and deliver a new Call Centre strategy for the incumbent Telecommunications company. With great power comes great responsibility.

Because I was contracting, as a self-employed individual, I was responsible for my own taxation and accounting. This was foreign territory for me.

I was subject to 'Provisional Tax', which meant that the Inland Revenue Service assessed my future earnings' and issued me with a tax claim in advance of my earnings. Even though once the initial project concluded, I had transitioned into a salaried role as General Manager for another company, I was desperate for help.

Kay told me to speak to her brother, David, who was a self-employed business owner in the logistics and transportation sector. David, in turn, recommended that I speak to his accountant, Clive Ellis. I am forever grateful to

Clive who got me out of the financial pickle that I had landed myself into.

Clive quickly reversed my situation and bought me the time that I needed. Whenever I came to see Clive, he would remind me that I needed to diversify. When Clive said, "Diversify", I knew that this was code for "Join Amway". What you need to know was that his garage was stocked full of SA8 and LOC (stable Amway cleaning products back in 1998), and the shelves in his waiting room were also stocked to overflowing with more Amway product. Despite his best efforts, I resisted his 'altar-call'.

Clive was persistent. At one time he offered me a series of three cassette tapes and encouraged me to listen to them. Each time we would meet, he would ask me whether I had listened to the tapes. I kept making excuses as to why I hadn't managed to listen to them. I had no intention of listening to them. In fact, they were rattling in the glove compartment of my company car. I preferred to listen to the CDs that I valued above those old-fashioned cassettes.

During one visit, Clive, instead of asking me if I had listened to the tapes, announced that he needed them back by the following Thursday as he had promised to loan them to someone else. I assured Clive that I would have listened to them before I returned them to him on Thursday.

Now I knew that when Clive received the tapes back from me that he would ask me what I thought of the content and what I had learned. I was snookered! I needed to listen to them.

With a sense of defeat, I popped the first cassette into the player and the dulcet Southern drawl of an American gentleman filled the atmosphere. He talked about sales in a motivational way that I had never heard of before. His name was Zig Ziglar.

I was so impressed with what I heard that I was impatient to hear the second tape. This contained a message on leadership that inspired me even more. The speaker was Dr. John C. Maxwell. My head was spinning, and I was eager to listen to the last tape. I ejected one tape and replaced it with the other. This was the message that would alter my life...

WHY IS IT RELEVANT TO CONNECT TO JOHN MAXWELL AND THE 21 IRREFUTABLE LAWS OF LEADERSHIP?

Skip Ross is the owner, founder, and director of Circle A Ranch. He and his wife Susan have dedicated their lives to making a difference in the development of teens through this ministry, and have spent over 40 years giving their summers to the work of Circle A.

Skip is author of the books 'Say Yes to Your Potential' and 'Daily Disciplines', and has created the 'Dynamic Living Seminar' and the 'Thrive Study Series'. He has traveled the globe teaching the principles of attitude development and leadership to millions of people for over 50 years. He has also recorded numerous audio and video teachings that have been distributed around the world with the help of Network 21 (the support partner to our Amway business) and podcasts.

He was the speaker on tape number three.

His message was on hope and forgiveness. He said that we fill our lives up with a multitude of items to keep us busy and fill in a void if it exists. For example, say that you had a wardrobe full of clothes that was crammed to overflowing. The chances are that you had a number of clothes that you wore regularly, and the rest just gathered dust as they stayed on their hangers untouched from day to day.

If you took the clothes that you never wore and took them to a 'charity shop' and recycled them, your wardrobe would most likely seem empty. Like a vacuum that needs to be filled, you would soon replenish the empty coat hangers with a new selection of clothes. The temporarily empty wardrobe would soon be bursting at the seams again.

There is always a need to fill a void and we need Jesus to help us do that.

Jesus, Skip went on to say, taught us to say the Lord's Prayer. In it, Jesus taught us as follows:

> *"This, then, is how you should pray:*
> *'Our Father in heaven,*
> *hallowed be your name,*
> *your kingdom come,*
> *your will be done,*
> *on earth as it is in heaven.*
> *Give us today our daily bread.*

> *And forgive us our debts,*
> *as we also have forgiven our debtors.*
> *And lead us not into temptation,*
> *but deliver us from the evil one."*
> (Matthew 6:9-13, NIV)

Forgiveness became a focal point of this prayer. Jesus said,

> *"...and forgive us our debts, as we also have forgiven our debtors."*

Skip went on to explain that when we choose not to forgive someone, it was the equivalent of eating poison, but expecting the other person to die!

These words pierced my heart. Inexplicably, tears started to flow down my cheeks as I realized that he was speaking directly to me. Skip was challenging me to forgive my father and my mother and to stop eating that poison that was killing me.

It was at that point in 1998 that I had my life-changing revelation about my relationship with my parents. It came some six-and-a-half years prior to my salvation, but it was an important first step that I needed to take on my road to redemption.

By July the following year, I found myself in Sydney airport, heading over to Melbourne with two cards in my hand.

In the first I wrote a message to my father, asking him to forgive me for my behavior towards him and telling him that I forgave him for everything that I had perceived that he had done to me. The second card I wrote to my mum, also seeking her forgiveness and forgiving her for my perceptions of her behavior that I felt had hindered my life.

There was a feeling of cathartic relief as I finished each card and I posted them from the airport. At last, after nearly 30 years, I was able to release the burden that I had been carrying thanks to a lie that I had believed. Finally, my life was about to start afresh...

WHY IS IT RELEVANT TO CONNECT TO JOHN MAXWELL AND THE 21 IRREFUTABLE LAWS OF LEADERSHIP?

I first saw John Maxwell speak in Newcastle, Australia in 1998. He had just released his book "The 21 Irrefutable Laws of Leadership". I sat in the audience like a hypnotized deer caught in the headlights, absorbing every word that he delivered.

This book, alongside the accompanying workbook, videos and audio material that he sold us from stage became my second bible.

I had just completed a role as General Manager for a car leasing company and was transitioning into the leadership role within a 45-seat call center. There were over 60 people reporting to me.

It was a Direct Response TV (DRTV) advertising company. We managed the majority of infomercials that came to TV. Some of you might recognize us as the "As Seen On TV" company. The trouble was that I had never managed a call center before, and I had no understanding of the new industry that I had joined.

I found out that at least one member of my team had unsuccessfully applied for my role, so I suspected that I had my work cut out for me.

In the original edition of his book, Maxwell included a law called "The Law of E. F. Hutton". In this law, Maxwell explained that "When the real leader speaks, people listen."

Many years ago, in the USA, there was a financial services company called E. F. Hutton. Their motto was "When E. F. Hutton speaks, people listen." This was amplified through one of their TV adverts. The setting was typically in a busy restaurant or other public place. Two people would be talking about financial matters, and the first person would repeat something that his or her financial broker had said about a particular investment.

The second person would say something along the lines of, "Well my broker at E. F. Hutton says..." At this point, every single person in the restaurant would stop what they were doing and turn around to listen to what the second person was about to say.

Who is your E. F. Hutton?

Before I started at the call center, I asked my employers if I could have a meeting with the team that I would be leading. I thought that it would be a good idea for them to meet me in person before I began.

I was ushered into the board room and sat at the head of the rectangular table, at the opposite end of the room to the door. A few minutes later the call center team filed into the room, filling the void between me and the door. I scanned the people as they entered and studied their body language. A few made eye contact with me, but the majority either stared at their feet or towards some invisible object that hovered a few feet above their foreheads.

The door was still open and I sensed that we were awaiting the arrival of another member of the team. With the sound of a clock ticking in my ears, I waited for what I perceived was nearly 5 minutes before a lady joined us and closed the door behind her. At this point, everybody in the room visibly turned towards her and directed their eyes in her direction.

Her name was Carol and she was my "Claude".

Maxwell shares the story of coming in to lead a rural Church in Indiana. During his first board meeting, he found himself leading a group of people whose average age was about fifty. Maxwell was a sprightly twenty-two! Assuming that he was the appointed leader, Maxwell believed that everyone would follow him because of his title.

As the meeting started, there was a brief pause, before a gentleman, in his sixties, named Claude cleared his throat and said, "I've got something."

"Go right ahead," Maxwell said.

"Well," said Claude, "I've noticed lately that the piano seems to be out of tune when it's played in the service."

"You know, I've noticed the same thing," said another one of the board members.

"I make a motion that we spend the money to get a piano tuner to come out from Louisville and take care of it," said Claude.

Soon others started to agree with Claude's idea and his motion was seconded and finally passed. That was the day that Maxwell realized who the real leader was in the Church. He may have held the position, but Claude held the power.

Are you developing relationships with your Carols and Claudes?

In my case, Carol held the power within the call center that I was about to

WHY IS IT RELEVANT TO CONNECT TO JOHN MAXWELL AND THE 21 IRREFUTABLE LAWS OF LEADERSHIP?

lead.

After our meeting, I asked Carol if she could stay behind and spend a few minutes with me. Alone, I thanked her for her contributions to the meeting. Soon she confirmed that she had applied for my role. When I asked her what her longer-term plans were, she told me that she would be looking to move on within six to eight weeks.

Then I asked her, what I perceived to be the most powerful question that I could conjure up. "What could I do to add value to your journey?"

Carol paused and thought deeply before she responded. "You can teach me more about leadership."

I told Carol that I respected her and the trust that the team had with her. I wanted to work with Carol and to learn as much as I could from her about how the systems worked, what she knew about each person – their strengths and weaknesses – and to see what she would have done to change things if she was leading this team.

In return, I would edify her to the team and teach her as much as she wanted to learn about leadership in her remaining time in the company.

This was a fantastic, synergistic relationship that helped both of us.

Maxwell became my mentor over the years. I devoured every book that he published and acquired as many of his tapes and CDs that I could lay my hands on. This helped to fuel my leadership journey.

In 2008, the New Zealand general election was held on the 8th of November. This would determine the composition of the 49th New Zealand Parliament. As the President of the Family Party, I wish that I could write that we celebrated our victory deep into the night, but alas, the results did not go our way.

I collapsed in exhaustion upon the conclusion of our campaign. Someone once asked me what it was like. I explained that it was a 9-to-5 job, meaning that it was a 9am start with a 5am finish! When asked if I would ever do it again, I replied only with a dozen good people at my side and $1,000,000 in the bank!

During 2009 I made the decision not to return to the corporate world, but to consult and contract with a couple of organizations. By August, I felt the urge to start a leadership training company and The Insight & Strategy Group was birthed. Running a year-long leadership program for a select number of clients, I felt the life flowing through my veins again.

Leaning on Maxwell's 21 Irrefutable Laws of Leadership, I mixed in my own content to create a pathway that my clients could forge.

At the conclusion of the program in 2010, one of the delegates would come and see me each month for some coaching. At the end of each session, he would encourage me to reach out to John and to see how I could partner with him. For months, I rejected this notion. For months, he persisted in reminding me of this idea.

Eventually, I succumbed to this preposterous idea and started my research. I remember John always talking about his Executive Assistant, Linda Eggers. In sales, it is better that you go through the gatekeeper, so I managed to locate an email address for her.

Late into the evening, I toiled as I drafted up an email expressing my desire to work alongside John and to partner with him. I gave her a breakdown of my background and the path that God had me traveling on. Only when I was happy with the structure and content of the email, I released it to the ether after I prayed over it, before leaving my office and heading off to bed.

The following morning, when I woke up, I saw that I had received a response from Linda. It took her less than an hour to reply to my email! She pointed me towards some individuals and organizations in the region that she thought might be able to help. Then Linda signed off her email steering me to a new resource that John was producing called 'A Minute with Maxwell.'

There is a song called 'Impossible' by the Christian band Building 429. However, in the lyrics they sing that there is no such thing as impossible.

WHY IS IT RELEVANT TO CONNECT TO JOHN MAXWELL AND THE 21 IRREFUTABLE LAWS OF LEADERSHIP?

*Nothing is unreachable
when we trust our God of miracles.
It takes a little to see and believe
that we can rise above the typical
and be anything but usual.*
(Lyrics by Building 429.)

I subscribed to the Minute with Maxwell and soon would wake up to the daily, minute-long, motivational message. One day, towards the end of February 2011, John mentioned that he was about to make a special announcement. The only information available related to the date of the announcement. With the date set in March 2011, I registered my interest.

The conference call, which was hosted by Paul Martinelli, introduced the concept of the John Maxwell Team (JMT). The vision was that we might be able to get the JMT to the dizzy heights of one thousand members. The invitation to apply to join the JMT was placed in front of us.

At that particular moment in time, the investment of US$5,000 seemed like a pipe dream. I may have been asset rich, but I was cash poor. It had been nearly 3 years since I left the corporate world and my income stream had not caught up with my previous vocation. After a year volunteering with the Family Party, and two years grafting to establish my business, I needed my miracle.

When I told Kay about the opportunity, I probably had a high level of anxiety in my voice. I was convinced that all 1,000 places would be snapped up in the first couple of days following the announcement. But we simply didn't have the funds necessary to make this happen. We closed off our call with a prayer. And we simply handed the opportunity over to God.

About an hour later I received a phone call. It was a loan officer at my bank. She wanted to apologize for the delay in getting back to me. A few weeks earlier I had applied for a bank loan to help me expand my business. But, due to the lack of communication, I had assumed that my application had been rejected.

Her call was to confirm that my application had been accepted! Once details were confirmed and paperwork was completed, I called Kay to tell her the good news.

My application to join the JMT was approved within 24 hours.

Today the JMT program boasts a 5-star Trustpilot rating, with over 24,000 John Maxwell Team members.

I have had the privilege of being personally mentored by John and my involvement expanded to include the development of the YouthMAX program and a seat on the PAC (Presidential Advisory Council) when it was formed in 2013. I am forever indebted to Paul, John and Scott M. Fay (the original Vice President of the JMT) for their support and belief in me.

As Paul Martinelli would remind us, "Jump and your wings will appear!"

I attended my first International Maxwell Certification (IMC) in August 2011. We packed out the room with 500 Founding Members at the Marriott, West Palm Beach. This was the first event and they grouped us alphabetically. I shared a table with Ed, Eddie, Edward, Elizabeth and, Francis. Hey, none of us knew any better back then!

As a bonus, we received an extra day of teaching from Maxwell. He shared 'The Five Levels of Leadership' with us. I'm not entirely sure that I could tell you much about the content in his teaching. But there was one thing that struck me in the message that he shared.

Maxwell explained that he was delivering his material in China, to the business and government leaders. At the end of his session, one of the organizers came up to Maxwell on the stage and said the following. "Dr. Maxwell, we have never heard leadership taught like that. Where do you source your material from?"

Maxwell responded that they didn't want to ask. They insisted that he share his source.

Again, Maxwell said, "You'll be disappointed. Don't ask."

The audience were unwilling to take no for an answer. Under pressure, Maxwell responded, "I source my material from the Bible." In unison, he saw their shoulders slump at the revelation of his source.

"I'm a man of faith," Maxwell explained. "If you want to come and talk to me about my faith, please come and see me after dinner. I'll be here in this corner of the room, ready to answer your questions."

After dinner a queue formed. It traced itself along the wall and through the door, snaking into the corridor with Chinese influencers keen to find out more.

Maxwell taught me more in this one story than through the cumulative content of his best-selling books.

As a man of faith, I have the opportunity to bring Jesus into the conversation at any time that I desire. If I choose to, I can verbally assault my audience with information about God and Jesus. (We called this bible-bashing when I was growing up in the UK.) Or I can introduce Him and the topic without offense.

Here are a couple of examples of how I can do this:

> *"As a man of faith, I would not be true to my beliefs if I didn't share the following..."*
> *"Let me tell you something about my faith. It is not my intent to force my faith on you, so please allow me to share the following..."*
> *"An old Jewish proverb says..."*
> *"One of my most cherished pieces of ancient wisdom is revealed in a story that Jesus shared..."*

If you, the reader, are a person of faith, how do you share your testimony about the wonders that God has done in your life? Are you hiding your light under a bushel or shining it for all to see? There are many ways and opportunities to share the Word. After all, it became the greatest commission from Jesus as He left the earth and ascended to heaven. He charged His disciples with a task that Christians today continue to work towards: "Go into the whole world and proclaim the good news to every creature."

I think that it was Saint Francis of Assisi who once said, "Go out there and preach the gospel, and if you need to, use words!"

TIME TO REFLECT...

What are some of the learning lessons in this experience?

Are you an E. F. Hutton? If you are not, then who is the person that speaks into your life?

From an early age I was a leader. The trouble was that I couldn't see that aspect within my life. I needed to learn the aspects of leadership from John Maxwell. I also learned that it was important to understand what it means to be a Christian in business.

I was living a life where I had a significant void. I sense that a number of readers might also have (or have had) a void in their life. What are you using to fill that void?

As I discovered in the last chapter, God was willing to forgive and forget all of my sins.

But before I got too carried away, I had to forgive others. Whatever your circumstances, are there people in your life that you need to forgive? Go back and read the Lord's prayer in Matthew 6:9-13. Meditate on what God is telling you, especially when it comes to the area of forgiveness.

Remember that unforgiveness is like eating poison but expecting the other person to die.

LEVERAGING GOD

CHAPTER SEVEN

What is your calling?

—————

When I returned to re-audit with the John Maxwell Team (JMT) at one of our International Maxwell Certification (IMC) events in 2014, we had outgrown our original venue and we transferred to the Marriott World Hotel, in Orlando, Florida. The room was set up to hold over 1,000 delegates. People were allocated table numbers that were selected not by alphabetical sequences, but according to their arrival time.

Each table had a leader or two who were there to mentor their peers, encouraging them the whole way. We also changed the format of the post IMC events. For the first time, we had an additional day of training that we could choose to invest in. That year they offered us training on selling from the stage.

I sat beside Denis Gianoutsos, my fellow "JMTer" from New Zealand during this program. Denis and I went back some twenty years through our mutual friends, Simon and Yvonne Godfrey. We analyzed the methodologies used and projected their suitability to the New Zealand-based audiences that we would encounter.

The Speakers on the stage started to build up the value of the Empowerment Mentoring program that they were pitching at us. This program was designed to help Coaches and Trainers to take an 'out of the box' program that they could use within their own business. It included scripted material to use on teaching calls. There were social media memes that were prepared for our immediate use. Handout material was prepared for our delegates and packaged up for our convenience.

By using the 'stacking' technique, they itemized the individual value of each item that the audience could buy in to. Soon it became apparent that the overall value of the offer was close to $19,500. I looked at Denis and he looked back at me. Between us, we anticipated that the 'pitch' would be that we would receive an 'offer' from the stage that would be in the region of $5,000.

We were not disappointed, nor surprised when that investment figure was revealed.

Before the final call to action came from the stage, establishing the trigger for the audience to rush to the back of the room to empty their wallets, Denis and I made the following observation. For us to be successful in our own businesses, we needed to find our authentic voice! Leveraging the wording given to us through the Empowerment Mentoring program would not make us successful.

Sometimes in life you get offered a job that seems right for you. But once you get into it, you soon find that it doesn't resonate with you and your values. Doing that job over a period of time starts grating on your soul, causing you to get restless and look for alternatives. How many of us have found ourselves in that situation? Before you jump into your next job, ask yourself if it is aligned to your authentic voice. Unfortunately, for Denis and me, the Empowerment Mentoring program included scripting that was not our authentic voice.

Who has held you back?

I have looked at my business and seen what I've tried to do via the business cards that I have produced.

I started off as the "Director and Principal Consultant" in the Insight &

Strategy Group. Soon that morphed into the "Forensic Consultant and Sniffer Dog". I know! What was I thinking?

Over time I moved into "Transitioning World Changers" before I became the "Jail Breaker". Finally, I transitioned to "The Corporate Counter Terrorist..." where I help CEOs and their teams introduce T.R.U.S.T. as a business currency as they start Disarming Corporate Terrorists...

If you're saying to yourself, "Really, Elias? What were you thinking?" I'd have to agree with you.

As I was navigating this territory, I went far and wide to seek my counsel. I talked to my peers within the Professional Speaking tribe. The trouble was that I had no discernment. I would talk to people who were unequally yoked with me.

At one stage, I remember being coached by a person, whom I later found out was an atheist. They questioned me about my faith and asked me whether I was targeting Christians or non-Christians. The reason that I was asked that question was driven by the fact that I had portrait pictures of myself dressed in overtly Christian clothing. Diamante crosses that covered 70% of the shirts were the giveaway.

As I pondered the question, I replied that I wanted to work within the Corporate world. Therefore, I was advised that I needed to drop my Christian outlook and blend in with the crowd.

In my book, "Liberating your Leadership Potential" I shared a story about the value of being equally yoked and selecting your mentors. Making the big move and giving up my corporate job with all its trappings seemed like the right thing to do at that time.

Starting up my own business proved to be one of the hardest. With no defined income, no clients waiting in the wings, and no products to sell, I created a challenge for myself!

During the start-up phase, I came across an opportunity to launch something called 'Leadercast'. It was a whole day leadership training program, featuring a number of presenters, including Jim Collins (author of 'Good to

Great' and 'How the Mighty Fall') and my personal mentor and leadership guru, Dr. John C. Maxwell.

The presenters were certainly top draw cards and respected in their individual fields. The challenge was that the Leadercast format was not known in New Zealand. The potential cost for me to promote the event was $30,000 – and I only had three weeks to make a go/no-go decision as to whether I invested the money (which I didn't have) and risk my marriage if it failed.

In his book 'The 21 Irrefutable Laws of Leadership', John Maxwell identifies The Law of the Inner Circle. Maxwell goes on to say, "Nobody does anything great alone. Leaders do not succeed alone. A leader's potential is determined by those closest to him. What makes the difference is the leader's inner circle."

What I believe Maxwell is saying here directly applies to us as leaders within our own businesses. Whom do we go to for guidance on the topics that require an external and objective perspective?

In my case, I needed to make sure I didn't make a critical decision in isolation. I ended up identifying five key people whom I approached to become my personal board of directors. The people I chose were identified based on two key criteria:

1) Their business acumen
2) Their spiritual oversight

I chose to meet up with them individually over coffee and ran the ideas past them. Then I invited them to join me in a group meeting where I laid out the opportunity I had.

And the result of that meeting...? I ended up with nineteen critical questions to ask the organizer that I had not considered previously! By the time I received the answers, I reported back to my inner circle, and the advice given to me by all five was not to proceed with the Leadercast program at that point in time.

I believe that exercise helped me to save my business and my marriage.

WHAT IS YOUR CALLING?

I have a simple question for you, "If you have a calling, who is calling you?"

I was recently introduced to Steven French. He authored a book called "The Jesus Journey". His book makes for compelling reading and is the foundation of the Lifework Leadership program.

In his book, French challenges the reader by stating that there is no calling without a caller. He goes on to write:

> *"God was the one who called Jesus. God called Jesus to particular actions, such as baptism, and to a particular leadership style that we will explore in this book. All of Jesus' choices came from his response to God's call, which was nothing short of complete submission. Jesus recognized God's voice, and he followed it. What voices do you listen to?"*

French talks about having a primary calling and a secondary calling. Our primary calling is to follow Jesus. The question is, "What is your secondary calling?"

To help you clarify this question, French points out that it relates to "where" you follow Jesus and "what" you do when you get there. Do we, as followers of Jesus, get relegated to a life in ministry, or can you do something that takes your talents outside of the Church?

According to the voices that I was listening to, there was no 'secondary calling' that could allow me to take my talents and preach the gospel in the marketplace.

There is some ancient Jewish wisdom that was shared in a story that appears in 1 Kings 19:11-13. It relates to God's revelation to Elijah. Whilst I refer to this story in my introduction, I would like to share it once more with you here:

> [11] *Then He said, "Go out, and stand on the mountain before the Lord." And behold, the Lord passed by, and a great and strong wind tore into the mountains and broke the rocks in pieces before the Lord, but the Lord was not in the wind; and after the wind an earthquake, but the Lord was not in the earthquake;* [12] *and after the earthquake*

*a fire, but the Lord was not in the fire; and after the fire a still small voice. *¹³*So it was, when Elijah heard it, that he wrapped his face in his mantle and went out and stood in the entrance of the cave. Suddenly a voice came to him, and said, "What are you doing here, Elijah?"*
(1 Kings 19:11-13, NKJV)

Luckily for me, I was able to hear the still quiet voice of God that told me otherwise...

What do the following numbers represent?
2.7 years.
961 days.
23,069 hours.
1,384,128 seconds...
These were the numbers that I was inheriting as I prepared to lead the Global Speakers Federation (GSF) during the year that I served.

As we finished our AGM and Board meeting for the GSF in July 2018, we had a ticking timebomb staring us in the face. With the expenditure rate outstripping our revenues, we realized that it was a matter of time before we would need to close the doors and end the journey that started in July 1997.

We recognized that the previous three years had been turbulent ones for the GSF, with the move from Council to Board (which included a re-write of our bylaws and policies) and the rebranding of the Global Speaking Fellow (from the older CSPGlobal). These initiatives had been labor-intensive and had consumed a lot of resources from our leadership team and Bond Exec as our Association Management Company.

In addition, on the positive side, there had been the introduction and welcome of three new Associations to our fold – Professional Speaking Association of Namibia (PSAN), the National Speakers Association of Sweden (NSA Sweden) and the Philippines Association of Professional Speakers (PAPS).

Towards the end of 2018 and the start of 2019, whilst I was celebrating my

20th wedding anniversary in Canada and the USA, I made a conscious decision that I was going to make 2019 a year of change.

I realized that my role as President of the GSF would be coming to an end in July. Having inherited the leadership of an organization that was losing money, I sought guidance from God and the Holy Spirit. I searched for scripture that would help guide me.

One day, as I read my Bible, I came across the following scripture:

> [28] *"Suppose one of you wants to build a tower. Won't you first sit down and estimate the cost to see if you have enough money to complete it?* [29] *For if you lay the foundation and are not able to finish it, everyone who sees it will ridicule you,* [30] *saying, 'This person began to build and wasn't able to finish.'"*
> (Luke 14:28-30, NIV)

I didn't want to be the one of whom they said, "It was Elias who ran the GSF into the ground and made it bankrupt!"

As I continued reading the same chapter, the next verse spoke volumes to me:

> [31] *"Or suppose a king is about to go to war against another king. Won't he first sit down and consider whether he is able with ten thousand men to oppose the one coming against him with twenty thousand?* [32] *If he is not able, he will send a delegation while the other is still a long way off and will ask for terms of peace.* [33] *In the same way, those of you who do not give up everything you have cannot be my disciples."*
> (Luke 14:31-33, NIV)

I knew that we had to review our expenditure and determine how we could be better stewards of what we have been given.

During the year that you serve as President of the GSF, there is an expectation that you will travel the globe and attend as many of the conferences that our Members would be hosting. As I calculated my obligation, I could be spending as much as one-and-a-half weeks per month away overseas.

I could be visiting 15 countries, with the majority of my time concentrated between February and May. During that time, there were conferences in India, New Zealand, Australia, South Africa, Namibia, Singapore, Malaysia, Sweden, Holland and, France.

As I pondered on this scripture, I was drawn to one verse in particular:

> "In the same way, those of you who do not give up everything you have cannot be my disciples."
> (Luke 14:33, NIV)

I spoke with my closest colleagues on the Presidential Leadership Team (PLT) and sought their advice. I wanted to run some ideas past them. One of the obvious items to consider was the renegotiation of the fees with our Association Management Company. Our workload had become less labor-intensive, which helped us to justify a reduction in their fees.

What I then suggested flew in the face of tradition. I wanted to seek the counsel of others on reducing the Presidential travel budget as well.

You have to understand that we had maintained the same budget for close to 10 years. In the past, there were fewer Members within the GSF, and therefore, fewer conferences that need to be attended. To expect the President to attend ALL of the conferences on the calendar, it would require that the President funded their travel by supplementing the costs from their own pocket.

But, I asked, what if, instead of sending me all the way from New Zealand to go to Namibia and South Africa, or to Singapore and Malaysia, we sent in a proxy from the PLT? After all, our Immediate Past President lived in Singapore. Surely it made more sense to have her represent the PLT in Singapore and Malaysia than to send me over? Or we could send our President-Elect, who lived in Amsterdam to South Africa and Nambia, where he could catch a direct flight from Amsterdam? Surely this would be more cost-effective and a better use of our resources.

After gaining the PLT agreement, I socialised this concept amongst a number of my key influencers on the GSF Board. Soon we had agreement and the revised budgets were set and agreed.

WHAT IS YOUR CALLING?

I would become the first President of the GSF who made a conscious decision to give up the international travel that gave us such a high profile. This left me with the obvious obligation of New Zealand and Australia as the two conferences that I would be traveling to attend in person. Looking at the remaining conferences, I agreed that it would make sense to be interviewed and recorded for the Swedish conference and to provide a remote presentation (via the videoconference technology of Zoom) for the Indian conference. The rest I delegated to other PLT Members.

TIME TO REFLECT...

What are some of the learning lessons in this experience?

First off, what is your authentic voice? Spend some time with people who know you and ask them to help you identify your real passion.

Once you know your authentic voice, it should help you to identify your calling. For me it was about helping Christian business owners. But the path that I took did not lead me directly to serving my audience.

Finally, as Steven French asks, who is the caller? For me, I received my calling directly from God to become the President of the Global Speakers Federation.

Go back and read 1 Kings 19:11-13. What are the noises that are currently drowning out the voice of God? How can you hear the caller if you are constantly surrounded by 'white noise'?

Author Jim Collins, in his book "How the Mighty Fall" recommends that people put what he calls 'P.W.S.' (Personal White Space) into their calendar. It is a time where your phone is off. There are no distractions, the music is muted, and your laptop is closed. This may be as little as 5 minutes per day, an hour each month or three days at the end of the year. Whatever you choose, make this a habit that you can sustain.

Once this has happened, surround yourself with your Inner Circle (some will refer to them as your personal board of directors). Read Proverbs 27:17 and ponder how you can become sharper as the result of those that surround you.

CHAPTER EIGHT

What does a free man do with his time?

The decision to reduce travel helped me to remove an obligation for business travel during 2019. As we holidayed on the East Coast of the USA and celebrated Christmas 2018 with family, we ended up in the Secaucus/Meadowlands suburbs of New Jersey, a short bus ride away from the Port Authority Bus Terminal in the heart of New York City.

Catching up with close family friends, fellow Kiwis Ruth and Muzz, who were traveling in the US, we visited some of the landmarks in New York City. The wind was bitterly cold and we navigated the subway to get to and from our destinations. (OK, I think that it is safe to confess that my sense of direction might have been affected by the colder weather. Not once, but twice, I took the wrong subway and led my family on a merry dance. Thankfully, no human or animal was hurt in this experience. So, as the Americans say, "No harm, no foul!")

New York City was preparing for the New Year's Eve celebration and its associated revelers. The barricades started to appear, and the police were out in force, directing traffic and pedestrians alike. We traveled in on Sunday the

30th of December in the morning and attended the Hillsong Church service. The church was located on W34th Street. Close by, on the corner of W34th Street and 8th Avenue was the Tick Tock Diner, where we had a traditional New York lunch.

We walked throughout New York and went down to Central Park, visiting the shops and admired their window displays. By the late afternoon, we headed back to the Port Authority Bus Terminal and caught our bus back to Secaucus and settled into our hotel room.

New Year's Eve dawned, accompanied by the rain. It was torrential. We opted to stay in our hotel and repacked our bags in anticipation of an early flight for Kay and the kids to Orlando on New Year's Day. After a few hours sleep, the alarm sounded at 3:15am. Forcing ourselves out of bed, I helped Kay and the kids take their luggage to the waiting taxi and I waved them off to the airport.

Due to my travel schedule, I ended up with an additional day in New York. My plan was to travel back into New York and have lunch with another Kiwi couple that were also vacationing in the Big Apple.

By the time I arrived in New York, the crowds had dispersed. The barricades offered an echo of the masses who had overtaken Times Square to watch the ball drop and usher in the New Year. Only the broken and disfigured umbrellas that occasionally littered the sidewalk gave any indication that there had been revelers here in the torrential rain a mere 12 hours earlier.

Over lunch, the conversation ventured on to the topic of New Year's resolutions and goals. When I was asked what my goal was for 2019, I paused and thought about my answer. After what seemed like an age, I responded that I wanted to use the experience gathered in the GSF within a CEO (Chief Executive Officer) role in New Zealand. After lunch, we headed our separate ways.

Fast forward to Tuesday, May the 21st, 2019. I received a call from my good friend and fellow speaker, Wynand Jacobs. We met through the Professional Speakers Association of New Zealand back in 2017. He is a very personable chap and we instantly connected.

WHAT DOES A FREE MAN DO WITH HIS TIME?

I found out that he had emigrated from South Africa with his wife and they were staying in accommodation located in Symonds Street. This was less than 4 kms from our venue. At the time Wynand utilized public transport, so I offered to give him a lift home after the meeting. It wasn't long before we established that we were both Christians.

As I parked my car to drop Wynand off, he asked me a simple question. "Elias, is there anything that you need prayer for?"

Thus, a ritual was started. Whenever I dropped him home after a meeting, we would park on the side of the road and pray for each other.

When his call came through, Wynand was excited about a new venture that he was exploring. He asked me whether there was a chance that we could meet up in town the following week. I checked my availability and then, on the off chance, said that I was popping in to see a colleague at the airport the following day. Was there any chance that Wynand was free to meet me on the Wednesday?

By divine appointment, Wynand chuckled as he explained that he had just had a cancellation in his calendar for lunchtime on Wednesday. Would I be able to meet him in town for a coffee? Once the arrangements were confirmed, he hung up the phone.

As I was parking my car in the carpark in town on Wednesday, my phone rang. It was Paul Adams. With the phone on hands-free mode, I reversed my car into the space.

Paul asked me if both Kay and I were coming to Church that evening? I confirmed that we were. His response was simple – he wanted to meet up with us both. I had used Paul as a reference for a CEO role that I had been shoulder tapped about. It was for a Christian organization called FamilyLife. The purpose of the meeting was to go through their extensive reference checks and he needed to clarify a few things with me and Kay prior to responding.

FamilyLife is a non-profit, faith-based, charitable trust committed to building strong marriages and families. It has been teaching, training and equipping families for over 25 years. As a result of their ministry, there are stories of husbands, wives, and children whose lives are different because of an interaction with something that FamilyLife has been part of. That's what FamilyLife is about; to inspire and equip couples to be successfully married for a lifetime.

From the conversation that I had with the person who recommended that I should apply, I felt that I was a shoo-in for the role. I had seen the Position Description, shared it with Kay in the hope that she might know someone who was suitable for the role. She told me that I should apply, which confirmed my thinking. Apparently, I was one of three people that was recommended by my friend to apply for the role.

I met Wynand and as we waited for our coffees to arrive, I asked him what the exciting project was that he wanted to talk to me about. Without any preamble, he asked me, "Have you heard of a Christian organization called Family Life?" I had déjà vu!

"Yes," I replied. "I have heard of them." Without elaborating, I asked Wynand to share more.

He explained how he had become aware that they were looking to recruit a new CEO for the organization, and he was applying for the role. Now I knew one of the other two people who were recommended by our mutual friend!

Wynand told me as much as he knew about FamilyLife and the recruitment process. He then told me that he wanted to talk to me about how I might be able to add value to him in the role, should he be successful in being selected.

Wynand was an ideal candidate for the role. Whilst in South Africa, he had authored a book on marriages. Titled, "Connection – A Journey Towards Intimacy: A 4-week devotional course with tools to build a strong and connected relationship", this showed his credentials in the area of marriage.

As he concluded his side of the conversation, I made a disclosure: I too had applied for the role of CEO at FamilyLife.

We shared our respective views of what Family Life needed and how best to help deliver on their vision and mandate. This was a ministry suited to couples.

Originally set up by Andy and Nikki Bray, this was an organization with an extensive history of making a difference in New Zealand. Their website was littered with pictures of couples on the "About Us" page.

WHAT DOES A FREE MAN DO WITH HIS TIME?

One of my main concerns about applying for the role was the fact that I would be involved in this role on my own. With her commitments at work, Kay was unable to join me in this ministry. It played on my mind how that would look... a marriage ministry that was being led by what looks like a single person.

The more I spoke to Wynand, the more it made me reflect on whether this was the role for me.

As we finished our coffee, I prayed for Wynand and he prayed for me. We embraced each other and went our separate ways to our respective meetings.

Later that evening, I arrived at Church in time to meet up with Paul. Kay and I sat down next to each other and Paul sat opposite us. He proceeded to tell us that he had been approached by the team at FamilyLife with a request to give them a reference for me. (I had put him down as a person who would represent me on behalf of City Impact Church.)

Considering that our relationship stretched back to 2005 and that we had worked together in the Family Party during the 2008 general election, I felt that he would be well placed to represent me. Paul said that when he received the reference forms and read through the extensive questions being asked, it rang some alarm bells for him. He contacted their office and requested a copy of the Position Description. As he read through it, he could see that I was very capable of fulfilling the role. But Adams felt that there was more.

"Elias," he said. "I know that you can do the job standing on your head. But this role is more than just a job. This is a calling. Can you please answer one question for me – is this your calling?" That was a great question. The short answer was, "No!" The long answer was, "Absolutely not!" No matter which way I looked at it, this wasn't my calling. I knew deep inside that Wynand was the right person for the role.

Paul asked Kay what her involvement would be, apart from supporting me in the role. She responded that she had no time to get involved beyond the emotional support that she could offer. As I suspected, this was something that I would need to deliver in isolation.

Kay and I thanked him and went home. We both knew that this opportunity would go no further.

The following day I contacted the person who introduced me to this role and explained where we had arrived in our thinking. With his blessing, I told him that I was going to withdraw my application as this wasn't my calling.

TIME TO REFLECT...

What are some of the learning lessons in this experience?

I had the skillset to fulfil the role as Executive Director at FamilyLife. That wasn't in doubt. By did I have the calling to do it?

Bob Buford wrote an interesting book called "Halftime: Moving from success to significance" and followed it up with "Game Plan: Winning strategies for the second half of your life". In Halftime, Buford reminds us that many people reach their 40s or 50s having completed their education, started their career, bought a house and often settling into marriage and raising a family. But they reach a crossroad where they start questioning their purpose in life.

His book focuses on this important time of transition – the time when, as he says, a person moves beyond the first half of the game of life. They are often catching a new vision for living the second half in a more rewarding way. If, as Buford states, your "...passion is to multiply all that God has given me, and in the process, give it back," then I encourage you to read his book.

CHAPTER NINE

What is your burden?

My spiritual journey restarted in 2005. As I mentioned earlier, my salvation at City Impact Church occurred in January of that year. The next logical step was for me and Kay to start attending as many activities as we could fit in at Church.

We were told that there was a mid-week prayer service as well as Sunday morning and evening services. The mid-week service was followed by a program called Gateway, that kicked off with an introduction to City Impact Church.

Gateway proved to be a valuable way to, not only find out more about the truth of the Bible, but also to knit us into the Church. We made many connections with the others who also journeyed through the Gateway program.

Soon we realized that between the Sunday services, the mid-week Gateway, business counseling with Simon and Yvonne as well as Kay's involvement with North Harbour Badminton, we were visiting the North Shore up to 5 times per week. At the time we were living in East Tamaki Heights, which provided us with a 45-minute commute each way (in good traffic) from the

South side of the bridge.

Inside a few weeks of committing ourselves to make City Impact Church our spiritual home, Kay and I made the decision that it would make sense for us to relocate to the Shore. We put our house on the market and, with the help of our fellow Gateway delegates, we prayed for God's blessing on the sale of our property.

A few days after selecting and engaging our Realtor (our Real Estate Agent), Kay left me with the kids as she flew off to Sedona in Arizona to attend her brother David's wedding.

We had our first Open Home whilst Kay was away. Within 24 hours the Realtor presented an offer for our property. There were three things that struck us:

1) The speed involved
2) The value of the offer broke the ceiling price for our street, and
3) The long settlement time (we had until the middle of April to find and move into a new home)

Looking back, I can see so many of God's fingerprints on this part of our journey.

When we found ourselves in the market for a new home, I knew what I was looking for. I could visualize the look and feel of the house, the number of bedrooms, the maturity of the garden, etc. The trouble was that I couldn't get Kay to 'see' the same things as me.

With pen and paper in hand, she sat me down and started to write out a list of what we were looking for: four bedrooms, a study, a separate dining area from the kitchen, a family room, the size of the land we were buying. The list kept growing...

Soon we were listing the suburb we wanted to live in and the proximity to motorways, schools, and shopping malls. Not a single detail was left out. By the time we counted them all up, the requirements totaled twenty-two. Then Kay and I added the twenty-third item to the list – the price we were willing to pay for the property.

Armed with the list in our hands, we started to visit Realtors in our desired suburbs. They were all impressed with the thoughtful detail we provided them. I suspect we represented a very small minority of their clientele. Unfortunately, most of them either burst into laughter or simply shook their heads when they finished reading our list.

"You'll never find a house for that price in this suburb!" they would chuckle.

Unsurprisingly, those that laughed didn't receive any commission cheques from us.

Having such an extensive list made the search easier – we could exclude certain properties without having to see them, which saved a lot of time! As time was running out for us and we had to vacate the house we had sold, we weren't tempted to buy the wrong house just to have somewhere to go – the list helped us to avoid a costly mistake.

We looked at over 50 houses. Nothing seemed to match up with our list. With time running out, we considered the option of renting. But even that pathway seemed to be blocked. At one point, we saw an advert for a property and called the Realtor on Friday afternoon to arrange a viewing. Much to my amusement, the Realtor advised that they only worked Monday to Friday and that we would have to wait until Monday to view it!

What does a person have to do to get some service around here?

With only four weeks before we were due to settle, Kay and I had one more roll of the die. It was Sunday morning and we went to Church in the morning with the kids, who were aged three and two at the time.

After the service, we picked up the weekly copy of the Real Estate listings and drove back over the bridge to go home. As I was driving, Kay scanned the listings and her eye was drawn to a full-page advert. A property, that we hadn't seen before had caught her eye. Circling it with a highlighter pen, she added it to the list of properties for us to consider and research when we got home.

There were a few challenges with this property.

First off, it was due to go to auction the following Saturday. This wasn't a good sign, as auction properties often meant that the price was uncertain and would probably be outside of our budget.

Secondly, it was in the suburb of Murrays Bay. This was one of the few suburbs on the East Coast Bays side of the North Shore that we had excluded.

By living there, we thought that we would be obliged to send our children to the local primary school. Kay's research indicated that it had received a poor Education Office Review, so we were sceptical about sending the kids there.

Finally, it was a massive house (approximately 300 sq. m.) which meant that, once again, it would probably be outside of our budget.

At home, when I looked it up online, I noticed that it was listed through the Ray White Real Estate Group. This was the same Realtors that we had sold our property through.

We were already linked into another Ray White Realtor who was helping us with our search on the Shore. I gave her a call and asked her if she could facilitate a private viewing for me that afternoon. When she recognized the property, she asked me if I was sure that I wanted to view it. In her eyes, she didn't think that I would like it. I told her to humor me and we set up a time to view this, and another property.

At the appointed time, I met her at the first property. The viewing didn't take too long as I soon discovered that the property wasn't at all suitable. We drove the 200 or 300 meters down the road and parked outside the second house.

It looks very unassuming from the street frontage. Please, do hear me properly. It had some street appeal, but nothing that was outstanding. She knocked on the door and it was opened by a teenager. (I would later find out that he was the eldest of seven kids, looking after the household whilst mum and dad were in Australia, finalizing the family move.)

As we entered the house, it expanded right in front of my eyes. It was a deceptively big house!

There were two bedrooms either side of an eleven-meter-long entrance hall. There was a third down the hall on the right-hand side, opposite a doorway that lead to the renovations below. As we walked past the bedrooms, there was a bathroom to the right, which marked off the end of the hallway.

To the left was a curved wall that extended, via a step-down, to a vast open-plan space. With a vaulted ceiling and a high stud, the room expanded into a kitchen and lounge.

The first level of the living area, that housed the kitchen, was another ten meters in length. The kitchen island was at least four-and-a-half meters long! It took my breath away.

The house kept on going. I walked the length of the kitchen and came to another step-down, which extended the living space by a further seven meters until we reached the three-meter-high French doors that separated the indoor and outdoor living. Outside I stepped onto a majestic deck that was bordered by a stainless-steel railing.

The Realtor and I walked to the edge of the deck to look out on to the secluded garden. We were at least five metres off the ground. I. Was. Blown. Away! And I hadn't seen the renovations downstairs.

As we retraced our steps and followed the breadcrumbs that led us back through the house, I started to notice things. There was a door that had been taken off its hinges (I later identified that it belonged to the doorframe that would eventually lead into Brianna's bedroom). It was being used as a temporary ping pong table for the benefit of the children's amusement.

In some of the rooms, electrical sockets were broken and in need of repair. Within the main bedroom, we had an ensuite, where damp towels littered the floor, abandoned by the little people who had last used them.

Rubbish spilled out of black refuse bags in the kitchen and filled the air with an unpleasant aroma.

I couldn't believe my eyes. Yet, despite its initial appearance, I was falling in love with this house with every step that I took.

We ventured downstairs, where we located a laundry, two more bedrooms, a lounge and bathroom in a self-contained space (with its independent entrance). I noticed cat dropping in one of the bedrooms, still exuding the aroma of a fresh deposit! And to top it off, there was a garage (I would later find out that it was a double garage) with boxes packed ready for the removal company to handle.

When we ventured out to the garden, I noticed that there was a little bridge that connected the two sides of the garden that were separated by a stormwater drain. This was a little inconvenient, I thought to myself. The bridge had no sides and could pose a hazard to my toddlers.

I knew, without any doubt, that I had found our forever home!

At the conclusion of my tour, I returned to the deck to peruse my kingdom. I inhaled and exhaled deeply before I called Kay to let her know what I had discovered. I tried my best not to oversell my hand and told her that I thought that she should come and view it. There were some issues, but not wanting to lead the witness, I didn't itemise my biggest fear of the stormwater drain.

Later that evening, Kay and I met up at Church and I told her more. She agreed that it sounded worth a viewing, which we arranged for Monday afternoon.

Like me, Kay instantly fell in love with the property. The water hazard, we both agreed, was something that we could manage through the erection of suitable fencing.

During my second viewing, I noticed that the curved 'feature wall' was painted in two different colors. It was apparent that the current owners were in the process of "cutting in" the wall, as they prepared it for painting.

Given the state of the place, and the amount of unfinished work, Kay wanted to get the security of understanding how much work would be needed to complete this project. I asked the Realtor if she knew any builders who she could recommend to produce a report for us. Given the state of the market at the time, and the proximity of the auction date, it was a long shot that we could get anybody to help with that.

As I dialed the number, I was pleasantly surprised to have it answered on the second ring. The builder, who introduced himself, asked me for more details. When I finished answering his question, he asked me when I needed this report back by. "This week?" was my optimistic reply.

"It must be your lucky day," he told me. "I just had a customer cancel their house inspection. Do you know if I can come and see the property on Wednesday?" With confirmation from the Realtor, we engaged the builder.

On Wednesday he visited the property. By Thursday he delivered a comprehensive report that detailed all the issues and remedial work that he recommended in vibrant technicolor. Now we knew the extent of the issues. Pictures accompanied each recommendation and we were armed with all the information that we needed.

I got on the phone to speak with Yvonne and brought her up to speed on where we were at with the property. She asked me when the auction was. I told her that it was in two days' time (Saturday afternoon). Straight away, she gave me the name of a leading auctioneer in Auckland and recommended that I call him.

The auctioneer took my call and told me that he was heading over to Waiheke Island on Saturday. Unfortunately, he wouldn't be able to help me on the day of the auction. But, if I could give him the address, he would do some research and he promised to get back to me on Friday.

By mid-day on Friday, he called me back and filled me in with some details. He told me how much the property had sold for in 2000 to a couple who started the renovation. It was originally built in the late 1950s. By 2000, they had demolished the back half of the house and added 230 sq. m. to the property. By all accounts, they ran out of money and love and eventually they separated.

The property was put back on the market in 2002 when the current owners purchased it for a disclosed amount. The auctioneer then proceeded to coach me on how the bidding process would work at the imminent auction.

Our first decision was to set – and hold fast to – a maximum budget that we were willing to pay for the property. The auctioneer would then ask for an opening bid. Under NO circumstances were we to put in the first bid. The auctioneer would have the ability to place an opening bid on behalf of the vendors. This would most likely be $100,000 below the reserve.

Once we knew what that was, we could start bidding. The strategy, it transpired, was to be confident and forceful with our bids. As soon as someone else placed a bid, we were to bid against it. The purpose was to frighten off other potential bidders until we became the 'last man standing'.

As he reminded me that I needed to stick to the original maximum bid, I thanked him for his help, and we hung up from each other.

That evening I received a call from my mum, who was living in Athens, Greece. She asked me how my search for a new home was progressing. I told her that we had found something that was coming to auction the following day.

Then my mum told me that she had a dream that she wanted to share with me. She told me that she saw a 'tall house' that we were going to buy. I was then quizzed in relation to the chattels that came with the house. (These are the fixtures and furnishing that the vendors leave behind.) I told her that it would most likely be the carpets and curtains etc.

"What about the kitchen?" mum asked.

I reiterated that they often leave the dishwasher and that would be it.

"You will also receive the fridge," she informed me.

I chuckled and told her that it was highly unlikely, as it was more common for the vendor to take the fridge when they left.

I love my mum, but really. A 'tall house'? With the fridge! I was highly dubious that it was within my future.

The next morning, I left the house early to travel to Ellerslie. I was invited by Simon and Yvonne to a fund-raising breakfast hosted by Peter Dunne, the leader of the United Future political party. That was where I would officially meet Paul Adams for the first time, who was then a member of parliament with United Future.

I was ushered to a table to sit beside Simon and Yvonne. On the same table, sitting next to me was Pastor Peter Mortlock, the senior pastor of City Impact Church and Paul next to him.

I told Simon and Yvonne what the auctioneer had told me. By now we were less than six hours away from the auction. When the breakfast concluded,

Yvonne spoke to Pastor Peter and asked him to pray for me and Kay and the forthcoming auction. I was the happy recipient of that prayer.

Driving home, I picked up Kay and we eventually met up with Simon and Yvonne an hour before the auction took place on site.

When we entered the property, we could smell the fresh paint. By some form of miracle, the curved feature wall had been painted a different colour and the whole house interior had a new lick of paint. With the auction being on-site, there were nearly 40 to 50 people in the house. Children were running wild and the number of adults were made up predominantly of the local neighbors, eager to get a sneak peek at the renovations (although we didn't know that until later).

Kay and I were registered as bidders for this auction. Kay stood to my left. Simon and Yvonne stood to my right. We stood with our backs to the curved feature wall.

The auctioneer gathered our attention and started to share instructions on the processes associated with this auction.

"The first change that I'd like to draw your attention to," the auctioneer said, "is that there is a change to the chattels. We will be including the fridge in this auction."

Goosebumps covered my arms and I held on to Kay's hand and looked quickly in her direction. Looking up to the high stud in the living area and towards the three-meter-high French windows, I realized that I was looking at the 'tall house' that my mother had dreamt about.

My heart started beating faster and I soon found myself with sweaty hands.

The auctioneer asked for an opening bid from the floor, but none emerged. He then proceeded to place an opening bid from the vendors. My heart sank as I realized that if that was $100,000 below the reserve, then we were at least $50,000 off the mark. We would never get to own this house.

I waited until the auctioneer asked if there was another bid, $10,000 higher than the opening bid he had created. Trained, as I had been the day before, I pounced and raised my paddle, placing my opening bid to the auctioneer. He tried to solicit another bid from the floor, but nobody else wanted to join his party.

As per his instructions, he then put the second of three bids on behalf of the vendors, raising the value by a further $10,000. "Do we have any other bidders out there?" he asked hopefully as he sought a further $10,000 increase. This was coming so close to our top bid.

Instinctively, my hand went up and my paddle registered us for the next bid. Kay squeezed my hand. My heart started to race, and my knees were knocking.

Kay leaned towards me and whispered in my ear, "Stop bidding! You're bidding against yourself!"

I felt like such a fool and I held my breath as I scanned the room to see if anybody else would join the bidding.

The auctioneer placed a last bid on behalf of the vendors and took the value up by a further $10,000. By this time, I managed to stop myself from unnecessarily bidding up the price of the property.

Without success, the auctioneer could get no further bids from the floor. He advised that the reserve had not been met and that he would be withdrawing the property from the market. As the highest bidder, I was invited to approach the auctioneer and enter into a private treaty.

Kay and I walked out to the deck and talked through our options. We spoke with our Realtor and asked her what our options were. She told us that the reserve was indeed set at the value that we suspected. After a short conversation, Kay and I agreed to meet the last bid, and our Realtor presented it to the auctioneer. He walked off to confer with the vendors and returned to let us know that they had rejected our offer. We thanked him and walked off the property and went home.

The next morning, Kay and I took the kids out to the park and played with them after Church.

We had talked further that previous evening about how much we liked the property and we showed our Realtor the builders report that detailed the amount of work that we were told was needed on the property. With the information that we had, Kay and I came up with a figure for a 'best and final' offer, which we asked the Realtor to present on our behalf.

"How much exactly did you want to offer?" our Realtor queried. We confirmed the exact value, which wasn't rounded to the nearest thousand dollars but ended with an unusual $88. Our rationale was that it would appear that we had completed our research and that this value would represent the maximum that we could stretch to.

If you have ever seen the reality TV program like Location, Location, Location, there is that uncomfortable time between placing an offer and receiving the call back from the Realtor confirming or denying your success. Our 'uncomfortable time' lasted less than 5 minutes. The incoming call ushered the good news that we were the owners of this house. Our unconventional offer was accepted!

TIME TO REFLECT...

What are some of the learning lessons in this experience?

As I unravel the web that we had spun, here is an analysis of what we discovered:

It is not our timing but His timing.

Though the desires are made in a man's heart, it is the Lord who directs his steps.

There is power in prayer.

Obedience will be rewarded.

Today I sit in my office, which is an extension that we built to our house, writing this book. We have lived here for nearly 15 years. The value that we purchased the house for, which was close to our maximum budget, was significantly less than the reserve price the vendors had set.

We have seen this investment nearly quadruple in value over a 15-year period. This is unheard of in any real estate market. Yet this is a blessing from the Lord that has enabled us to go from strength to strength.

CHAPTER TEN

Are you working in your own strength?

After we moved into our new home, we were fully committed within our Church. Well, when I say "we", I'm actually referring to Kay.

We attended the Gateway program, which ran for a total of twenty-four weeks, across three separate eight-week semesters. We were aware that at that time you had to graduate from Gateway before you were able to serve in a team.

Kay and I spoke about this and we agreed that I would drop out of Gateway before the start of the final trimester. This way, if I didn't graduate, then I couldn't serve. It was a simple, foolproof plan! I made up the excuse that I was busy at work and this helped me delay my graduation.

I thought that it was more important for me to focus on work and to grow our Amway business. Oh. how foolish I was...

Let me introduce you to a chap called Obed-Edom.

The story starts in the Old Testament of the Bible. David, God's chosen leader, has been crowned king of Israel. He has succeeded king Saul, Israel's first king, and gathered an army of thirty thousand able-bodied young men of

Israel. They enter battle with the Philistines in a place called Baal Perazim.

King David has the wisdom to enquire of God, "Shall I go and attack the Philistines? Will You deliver them into my hands?"

The Lord answers him, "Go, for I will surely deliver the Philistines into your hands."

OK. Here's a spoiler alert. Look away now if you don't want to learn something important! David sought counsel from God. He didn't try things in his own strength and assume that he knew all the answers. He humbled himself and sought out a higher wisdom.

Having defeated the Philistines, he then sent his troops to Baalah in Judah to bring up from there the ark of God. (Yes, this is the same ark that Indiana Jones fights the Germans for in the film Indiana Jones and the Raiders of the Lost Ark.)

Placing the ark on a cart, they had some oxen pull the cart as they relocated to Jerusalem. They made a real song and dance of this (literally!).

> *David and all Israel were celebrating with all their might before the Lord, with castanets, harps, lyres, timbrels, sistrums and cymbals.*
> (2 Samuel 6:5, NIV)

You can imagine the commotion that was created nearly 4,000 years ago. They are carrying this precious cargo on the back of a rickety cart, drawn by some oxen on the equivalent of an unsealed metal road. The sound of the crowd would have been deafening to the oxen and the uneven road would have posed a problem to the safety and integrity of the cargo.

They brought it from the house of Abinadab, which was on the hill. Uzzah and Ahio, sons of Abinadab, were guiding the new cart when all of a sudden, disaster struck. When they came to the threshing floor of Nakon, the oxen stumbled. To avert the impending disaster, Uzzah did what any red-blooded young man would do... he reached out to catch the ark before it fell.

It is documented that

> *"The LORD'S anger burned against Uzzah because of his irreverent act; therefore God struck him down, and he died there beside the ark of God."*
> (2 Samuel 6:7, NIV)

Harsh!

First, you have to be aware that God had given Moses and Aaron specific instructions about the Tent of Meeting and the movement of the Ark of the Covenant. In particular they were told that

> "...they shall not touch any holy thing, lest they die."
> (Numbers 4:15, NKJV)

OK, the lesson here is, "Don't mess with God!"

Unsure of how to proceed and wary of causing more death and destruction amongst his people, king David was unwilling to take it any further. So he makes a decision to leave it at the house of Obed-Edom the Gittite. (Side-bar note: Didn't they have the coolest names back then?)

I don't know about you, but if I had just witnessed the death of an impudent young man, who was struck down for trying to save the ark, I would have second thoughts about having the ark camped in my living room at home. I'm not sure that I would have had enough self-discipline to walk carefully around it at night as I navigated my way to the toilet in my frequent nighttime rituals. What if I accidentally bumped into the ark? What would happen to me and my household?

The answer is not what most people would think:

> "The ark of the Lord remained in the house of Obed-Edom the Gittite for three months, and the Lord blessed him and his entire household."
> (2 Samuel 6:11, NIV)

He was blessed? How could that be?

As my Uncle Costa would often tell us when I was growing up, "Elie-boy, this is one of the mysteries!" Everything could be explained away in the Bible by referring to it as a mystery!

Having witnessed the blessing that Obed-Edom and his household received, king David amplified his efforts to bring the ark back to Jerusalem.

In their second attempt, they had thought this through and came prepared. They were still dancing and singing, celebrating with the might of Israel behind them. Except, when those who were carrying the ark of the LORD had taken six steps, David sacrificed a bull and a fattened calf. I don't know about you, but I suspect that there was a lot of sacrificing going on during that journey!

And what happened to Obed-Edom? Did he and his household fade into insignificance and were they wiped off the face of the earth, smitten as many were before them?

There is an interesting observation by Richard Spangler, in his article "Who is Obed-Edom?" (https://www1.cbn.com/devotions/who-obed-edom)

> *When it came time to move the Ark to Jerusalem, (this time correctly) Obed-Edom had a choice. He could have stayed where he was and lived off of his past relationship with God or move with the Ark of God, staying in God's presence and in relationship with God.*
>
> *Obed-Edom had a desire for the Lord and moved with God. His desire for the Lord caused him to do whatever it took to be close to the Lord. He became a gatekeeper, a musician, and a doorkeeper for the Ark. Due to Obed-Edom's desire and love for the Lord and his faithfulness, God begins again to bless him and promote him.*
>
> *Obed-Edom becomes a worship leader and is mentioned along with Aspah the Chief Musician. Obed-Edom and his 68 associates minister regularly before the Lord in worship. Yet, he still continues to keep the gates.*
>
> *Obed-Edom is not only blessed in ministry and relationship with the Lord, his family is also blessed. God gives him eight sons, his poor wife raising a football team. His sons and grandsons also worshiped the Lord and were blessed by the Lord. They were all leaders, capable men, with strength to do the work. There were 62 men in all.*

Obed-Edom, along with his other duties, was put in charge of the Southgate and his sons were keepers of the storehouse.

Obed-Edom becomes one of the most referenced individuals in the Bible. Nineteen times, to be precise.

Obed-Edom and his household start to serve in the House of God, gaining as much proximity to the ark as they can get. Here are some of the tasks that they performed:
- Doorkeeper of the ark of the covenant
- Appointed to sound harps
- Appointed to minister before the ark of the covenant
- A doorkeeper of the temple
- A conservator of the vessels of the time in the time of Amaziah

And the list goes on.

If I had read and understood the story of Obed-Edom, I should have jumped at the opportunity to complete Gateway and serve in the team at City Impact Church. But I knew better, or so I thought...

―――

When the penny drops, so does the enemy.

It was at least a year before I made the decision to complete Gateway. I rejoined the team for the third intake and graduated eight weeks later. Kay had started to volunteer at Church and she had better insight into the individuals and their teams. I was encouraged to avoid Children's Church and to seek a role in the training team.

I was invited to have a consultation, where the Gateway graduates would meet up with a leader and be interviewed, with the objective of matching us up to a team that we could serve in. Armed with the advice that Kay gave me, I put my best foot forward and told my interviewer about my strengths and where I saw God using me most. I would be happy, I said, to do anything to support the trainers that delivered the Gateway program. Setting up the room, managing the projectors, playing the worship CD. Anything - except for the Children's Church!

Thankfully I was allocated to the Training Team and soon I was setting up the room, managing the projector and playing the worship CD. I found myself in my element, greeting the attendees and making them feel welcome.

TIME TO REFLECT...

What are some of the learning lessons in this experience?

When you get to serve God, you get blessed. I was going to say that you got a blessing, but it is not simply singular! Obed-Edom received multiple blessings.

If you are planted in a Church, don't put off serving for a later point in time – maybe one that is more 'convenient' for you. Start serving NOW!

It doesn't have to be in a Church. It could be where you work. At school. Or in your local community.

Maybe, like Obed-Edom, you want to get closer to God and get to know Him better. If the stories about Obed-Edom are true, the measure of your blessings could also be excessive!

CHAPTER ELEVEN

Why should you clean yourself with your daily S.O.A.P.?

"Do you know what B.I.B.L.E. stands for?" one of the trainers in my Gateway class asked. "It stands for 'Best Instruction Before Leaving Earth'!"

I concluded that I could do myself no harm in reading it from cover to cover. After all, I might read something that could help me in my personal relationships or with my work. It was well worth the effort.

One chapter from the Old Testament, one chapter from the New Testament; one chapter of Psalms, one chapter of Proverbs each day. By following this formula, I would cover the whole Bible in one year.

With 31 chapters, Proverbs was the easiest to keep track of. If it was the 5th of the month, it was Proverbs 5 that I would read. If it was the 6th, I would read Proverbs 6.

I was also told to read my Bible using the S.O.A.P. methodology.

S.O.A.P. is an acronym that stands for:
- Scripture;
- Observation;
- Application; and
- Prayer.

I made the decision to get started in this new discipline on a daily basis. With the purchase of a spiral-bound A5 notebook, I started to journal my thoughts and observations.

As I read through my four daily scriptures, I would look out for scripture that spoke to me and would write it down in the journal. Then I would document my observation as it related to that particular scripture and would follow that with a practical application as to how that would relate to me.

The process was complete by creating a prayer that I would use to help me integrate the scripture into my life.

With my Bible reading plan laid out on a piece of paper to my right and my Bible in front of me to the left, I opened it up and scanned through to the first scripture for that day – Isaiah 40.

Reading through the chapter, my eye was drawn to the last verse. I stopped to ponder what this meant.

As I thought this through, I picked up my pen and opened my journal to page one, where I wrote the following:

Day #1
SCRIPTURE: Isaiah 40:31, NKJV

> *But those who wait on the Lord shall renew their strength; They shall mount up with wings like eagles, They shall run and not be weary, They shall walk and not faint.*

OBSERVATION:

> *By reading this scripture it makes me feel as if un-ending energy could be mine if only I would "wait on the Lord". I believe that this statement means that I believe in Him and I praise Him and I do His will.*

APPLICATION:

> *My application of this in my life is by a number of realizable actions:*
> 1) *I could pray more often.*
> 2) *I could be filled with the Holy Spirit and rely on the Holy Spirit to lead me in my actions and interactions.*
> 3) *I could witness more often to people.*

PRAYER: My prayer:

"Thank You Lord Jesus for coming into my life & for the changes that you have affected upon my life. I pray that You fill me with the Holy Spirit & that You teach me how to rely on the Holy Spirit for guidance in my everyday interactions and transactions. I pray Lord that I will continue to gain strength from the influence of the Holy Spirit, that the Holy Spirit will sustain me & carry me effortlessly through my day & give me abundant strength & energy to help me fulfill Your will on earth."

And so my daily discipline began.

Every day I would get up early in the morning and dedicate up to an hour to reading my Bible and ruminating on the Word of God, waiting for scripture to drop into my heart. I was hungry to seek any wisdom that I could get and to pursue help, support and favor from God through my prayers. I already knew that if it was purely up to me and my own strength, I was never going to make forward progress.

Day #2
SCRIPTURE: Psalms 72:12, NKJV
For He will deliver the needy when he cries, The poor also, and him who has no helper.

OBSERVATION:
God will deliver everyone on earth. He has absolute power and control over our lives. He will deliver "him who has no helper." Even the helpless can be delivered by God. No matter how helpless (or hopeless) I feel, God will deliver me and reward me.

APPLICATION:
Whenever I feel helpless – that I'm losing, I'm drowning, I have self-doubt surfacing – this is the time to turn to God and ask Him for deliverance. I will pray to Him and I will praise Him.

PRAYER:

"Lord Jesus, I pray that when I feel times of inadequacy that I turn to You for guidance & deliverance. I pray Lord that You give me hope & guidance, Lord, as I search for ways to lift myself. I pray that You show me the way, give me the answers to help deliver me from my state of despair into a state of confidence. Lord Jesus, I pray that you lift me out of the pit that I find myself in."

Day #3
SCRIPTURE: Proverbs 25:16, NKJV
Have you found honey? Eat only as much as you need, Lest you be filled with it and vomit.

OBSERVATION:
Honey could represent praise and recognition for the work that I have done. Having too much recognition or praise could lead to big-headedness or ego.

APPLICATION:
I have to have a level of modesty with everything that I do. I need to share the "honey" with others, giving them the recognition and the rewards for their hard work.

PRAYER:

"Lord, I pray for humility in the things that I do. I praise You for the successes that I have in my life, my job & my business. It is Your will that I do. You determine my success & I cannot succeed without Your Holy Spirit leading me & guiding me each & every step. Lord, I pray that You will keep me grounded & humbled in every venture I undertake & give me the wisdom to recognize others & support them for the work they do & their contributions to my success. Lord, I edify You at every opportunity."

Day #4
SCRIPTURE: Isaiah 44:2-3, NKJV
Thus says the Lord who made you and formed you from the womb, who will help you: 'Fear not, O Jacob My servant; And you, Jeshurun, whom I have chosen. For I will pour water on him who is thirsty, and floods on the dry ground; I will pour My Spirit on your descendants, and My blessing on your offspring;

OBSERVATION:
God has chosen me even before I was born. He has named me and He knows me. He will feed me and water me - I'll never be thirsty. In a similar fashion, I'll never be hungry – The Lord will always provide for me. I'll always be blessed – as long as I diligently seek the Lord.

APPLICATION:
In the times of my drought – when I lack success at work or in my business – I know that the Lord will flood the dry grounds. He will pour His Spirit over me and into me to bless me when the timing is right.

PRAYER:
"Lord, I pray that You will look after me & my family. You have chosen us individually. You know me & You love me. I pray that You help me during this period of drought as I seek successes in my business, my job & my relationships. Lord, I ask for Your forgiveness & I seek Your blessing. I pray that You will let the floodgates open & that You cover my life with success. I pray Father for the quenching of my thirst. As You have promised, pour Your Spirit on me & my descendants & pour Your Blessings on us also. Lord Jesus, I pray for a breakthrough in our business & in my work & in

my relationships. Lord, I pray specifically for financial success and financial blessings in my endeavors. Lord, I pray for a breakthrough – for Your will to be done on earth as it is in heaven. I pray in the name of Jesus – who died on the cross to save us from sin with His blood."

Day #5
SCRIPTURE: Revelation 21:4, NKJV
And God will wipe away every tear from their eyes; there shall be no more death, nor sorrow, nor crying. There shall be no more pain, for the former things have passed away."

OBSERVATION:
The past is behind us. Once we know God, our past is forgiven and our hurts are behind us. We can forget the past and start again. We cannot be hurt because we are protected by God, through our belief.

APPLICATION:
I would often dwell on past failures and use them as roadblocks to current and future successes. Now that I know the Lord, I must learn to let go of the past and focus on the painless present and the perfect future.

PRAYER:
"Lord, I pray that You forgive me my past transgressions & sin. I thank You Lord for coming into my life & for forgiving me my sins. I pray Lord that You continue to bless me & my family. I thank You Lord for Your ever loving kindness that You can wipe away my pain & my tears. I pray that You help me to keep my focus on the present & the future that You have in store for me."

TIME TO REFLECT...

What are some of the learning lessons in this experience?

We need to be brainwashed! Not in a cult-type experience. But in a positive, let's-get-rid-of-the-rubbish type of experience.

Over time, we have seen, heard, and absorbed a number of messages and ideas that have become thought patterns. Not all of them are positive. (Just go back and review the chapter on "Your Secret Name"!)

Use the time to get into the habit of doing a daily S.O.A.P. program. Empower yourself by reading the Bible from cover to cover.

Analyse it and dive deeper into the word of God.

This will help you to reverse the negativity that might have become a stronghold in your life and replace it with the word of God.

LEVERAGING GOD

CHAPTER TWELVE

Is scripture more powerful than an airbag?

I took my car in to get its Warrant of Fitness (WOF) – only to have it fail the test.

"There's an obstruction to the airbag," the technician at the Testing Center told me.

Surely the man was having a laugh with me. There was absolutely no way that he could be serious, I thought to myself. Attached to my steering wheel was a 3 x 5 card with the following scripture written out:

> "But without faith it is impossible to please Him [God], for he who comes to God must believe that He is, and that He is a rewarder of those who diligently seek Him."
> (Hebrews 11:6, NKJV)

This got me thinking. Could it be that the technician was reacting to the scripture? But why would the Word of God create such an adverse reaction amongst some people, such that they would go to extremes to have it hidden from the masses?

I removed the card, which had been blue-tacked to the steering wheel, and re-submitted my car less than a minute later to the same technician for its WOF. Oddly enough, it passed with flying colors!

I promptly drove my car out of the testing station and reapplied the card to the steering wheel. The words spoke life into my situation and I knew that if I could apply this scripture to my life that the ultimate rewards would surely follow. I pulled up to the lights and waited for them to turn green.

My mind started to race. Ever since I was a young boy, I had always been a believer. I knew that there was a God in heaven that had created heaven and earth, and that He sent His only begotten Son down to earth so that He could die to save us from sin. I had attended Church regularly (some would say religiously) when I was growing up.

Belonging to a Greek Orthodox family, the Church had played a focal point in my family's life. My mother was involved with the choir and they would often come over to our house during the week to practice and prepare for the following week's service.

To me, this was an unusual custom. I observed the rehearsals and believed nothing had changed in nearly 2,000 years. On a Sunday, when I attended the Church service, I would know the routine off by heart. I knew when to stand and when to sit; when to bow my head and when to look back up; when to make the sign of the cross and when to kneel down.

It was a religious experience, right down to the annual 40-day fast over Easter.

My family would remove all dairy products from their diet during their fast. No eggs, cheese, milk or meat. No explanation was given, nor any education made available, to help me understand the rationale behind this practice.

In essence, this made it a religious experience and I never realised that the alternative was a relationship.

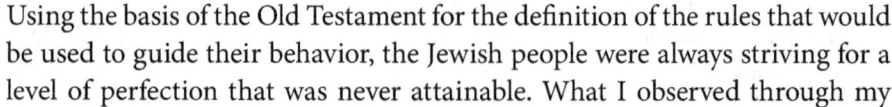

Using the basis of the Old Testament for the definition of the rules that would be used to guide their behavior, the Jewish people were always striving for a level of perfection that was never attainable. What I observed through my

IS SCRIPTURE MORE POWERFUL THAN AN AIRBAG?

attendance at the Greek Orthodox Church was that I found myself in a ritualistic environment. I would see the women segregated to one section of the Church and the men to another.

Occasionally a woman would be given the responsibility to read the scripture. But she had to have her head covered with a shawl before she could fulfill her obligations.

I never understood the need for the repetitive nature of the services. However, I was willing to go through the charade to be seen in the right light by the appropriate powers that be.

Yet, I would spend more time looking at the women and seeking out the more attractive ones in the congregation, trying to figure out who they were related to and whether they were married or single, rather than pay attention to the service.

I soon got disillusioned with the environment and over time stopped going to Church altogether. When I started living in New Zealand, I had a warped view of the Greek Orthodox Church that was mainly driven by a lack of education. I eventually started going back to Church in 2000 because Kay had wanted to attend a Christmas Carol service. We ended up at the local Anglican Church, where Kay and I began attending on a semi-regular basis.

Despite my prejudices, I found myself in an uplifting environment after I gave my life to the Lord. I received a broader viewpoint, which was accompanied by an education to explain the relevance of scripture – whether it appeared in the Old or the New Testament. I finally understood that there was a difference between religion and relationship. And it was religiosity that had turned me away from the church.

With these memories churning freshly over in my brain, I made sure the 3x5 card was secured back in place. I was grateful that I had finally understood the true meaning of Christianity and that I had developed a personal relationship with Jesus Christ.

I finally was able to understand that nothing that I did would be able to help me buy my way into heaven. No amount of 'works' would gain my salvation. It was a free gift that I had to claim. I realized that I was never going to be able to please God, because I was a human being, and with that came a flawed nature. I had a sinful nature and no number of laws and rules were going to rectify that fact.

I now understood the nature of the sacrifice that Jesus had endured on the cross, where His blood was shed to cover and redeem the sins that I had committed, and would no doubt continue to commit.

I had faith that God was real, and that God could provide me and my family with a better outcome whilst we lived here on earth. I was willing to diligently seek Him through a combination of prayer, Bible reading, and praise and worship.

The lights turned green, and I knew that God would reward me...

TIME TO REFLECT...

What are some of the learning lessons in this experience?

There is a difference between religion and relationship.

God created us for a relationship. In the garden of Eden, Adam and Eve lost that relationship with God after they disobeyed God and ate the fruit from the tree of knowledge of good and evil. (You can read more about this in Genesis 2.)

God is still looking to have a relationship with us. It can be as real as talking to your spouse or your colleagues at work or your children at home. Jesus demonstrated it so well during His ministry.

One of the greatest stories recorded is found in John 4:1-26, where Jesus connects with a woman at the well and strikes up a relationship with her. As a result, it not only transforms her, it also changes a city.

CHAPTER THIRTEEN

Do you have the full picture?

Kay enjoys doing jigsaw puzzles. This summer she purchased half a dozen second-hand puzzles from the local charity shop. I think that the smallest one weighed in at 1,000 pieces. The moment that the box is opened and its content spills out, I instantly get a shiver that runs down my spine!

As soon as I see the cacophony of color spill on the table, I break into a cold sweat. Pieces drown each other out and all that I can see is a kaleidoscope of colour that makes no sense to me.

Kay sits there patiently sifting through the pieces, organizing them into various categories.

The pieces with a straight edge.

The pieces with red in them.

The green and purple pieces.

And so on. To me, it looks like chaos. For Kay, it is organized chaos.

Kay has a system. It starts off by connecting and completing the border for the jigsaw. All the pieces with a straight edge serve one purpose – to create the frame that the jigsaw will sit in. Once this is completed, Kay gains a sense of the size of the puzzle (problem) that she has to work on.

I'm not sure if you have ever purchased and worked on a jigsaw puzzle before but let me share a few observations. Each puzzle box has a common item on the front. Have you guessed what it is? The answer is simple – a picture!

Kay makes sure that she can always see the picture of the finished puzzle. This gives her a reference point of what she is trying to create. Some would say that is cheating – but not me!

What picture are you looking at?

"What if I gave you the following task? I want you to pack a box with a ball and ship it out. You'll get paid $1,000 / box and you can do 500 boxes per day. Can you create $10M in revenue? Yes, in 20 days...."

This instruction was given to us by Pastor Gary Keesee on the 4th of August 2019.

How would you feel about making $10M in revenue? Maybe you are looking at your current situation and saying to yourself, "That's impossible! It is outside of my reach. I don't have the resources/patience/intelligence (fill in the appropriate word for your situation here) to make that happen."

Maybe you view $10M as a drop in the ocean. "Yes, I can do that," you say to yourself. "Where shall I start?"

Irrespective of which side of the coin you see, you need to have a starting point and a perspective.

Pastor Keesee continued to share a story with us. Jesus found himself standing by the Lake of Gennesaret preaching to a large crowd. To make it easier for Him to get His message across, Jesus spots a couple of boats, unused and drifting on the water. Jumping on to the one owned by Simon, Jesus commands him to put the boat out from the shore, where He proceeds to start preaching.

At the conclusion of His sermon, Jesus instructs Simon to take the boat out to go fishing.

Simon, who was an experienced fisherman had already toiled all night and caught nothing. I guess that he would be the equivalent of a Captain on one of the boats that is the focus of the TV series, "Deadliest Catch". Simon knows the water like the back of his hand. He was probably tired and frustrated, with nothing to show for his efforts.

And now, to add insult to injury, this man, Jesus, wants him to roll the dice one more time and go out to the deep. Simon is probably thinking, "Is He for real?"

Instead, Simon says, "But because you say so, I will let down the nets."

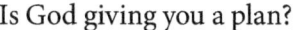

Is God giving you a plan?

You can always find fish if Jesus tells you where to go... The question to ask yourself, is where do I have to go to find the fish? It would help if you have a plan. That's something that I observe that Kay has with her jigsaw puzzles.

There are three things you must do to find a plan.
1) You must have the right picture. (Not of your failure and your past!)
2) Get the plan. (Ask God for His plan!)
3) You have to execute the plan! (It's very hard to steer a parked ship!)

Was it worth it for Simon to listen to Jesus? The next two verses show us the value of executing on good counsel:

> [6] "When they had done so, they caught such a large number of fish that their nets began to break. [7] So they signaled their partners in the other boat to come and help them, and they came and filled both boats so full that they began to sink."
> (Luke 5: 6-7, NIV)

"Their nets began to break." Imagine what the haul would have looked like! I suspect that Simon had rarely (if ever) seen a harvest of this magnitude. In fact, it was so big that Simon nearly lost his fleet as they filled the boats to overflowing, "so full that they began to sink."

If you are in business, you must be asking yourself, "Where do I need to go to find my tribe? What market sector must I focus on?" Whatever the questions are that you need to ask in relation to your situation, let me encourage you to ask God. He knows what is good for you and He is ready, willing and able to field your call.

Are there fish in the lake? If so, it might as well be me who gets them.

Our home is a short walk away from a number of beaches. Within five minutes you can be at Murrays Bay beach. Mairangi Bay and Rothesay Bay beaches are within 10 minutes' walk on either side of Murrays Bay.

Shortly after we moved in, Kay went for a walk at the local beach to spend some time talking to God. She came back with a glint in her eye. And that was when she dropped her bombshell on me.

"God told me to give up my career and look after the kids," she announced. "Really!" I squeaked, my voice breaking as the word was given life. I cleared my throat and with a more manly tone repeated "Really?"

At the time Kay was earning $125 per hour as a consultant. With our newly found faith, our financial commitments had changed. We had chosen to follow the Word of God and started to tithe 10% of our income to God. With this increased financial commitment, Kay's decision seemed to fly in the face of reason.

We could barely make ends meet and now Kay wanted to put further strain on our situation!

Within a week, the real test of faith started to kick in. I received a call from one of my customers.

"Hi Elias, it's John here," he announced. "I've got some good news for you. The board reviewed your proposal and they'd like to give you and the project the go-ahead. When can Kay start?"

"I think that Kay is on another assignment," I replied. "Let me check with her and I'll get right back to you."

I called Kay and laid out the opportunity in front of her. It was a 6-week assignment that was worth $40,000.

"What do you want me to tell John," I asked. "Are you going to say 'Yes' or 'No'?"

"No" was the only word Kay needed to say.

Once I stopped crying, I picked up the phone and called my client back.

"I'm sorry John, but as I suspected, Kay is working on another assignment and can't commit to your project. Leave it with me and I'll source another consultant to work with you."

Kay walked into the room and handed me a sheet of paper. "I've been looking at our budgets and I think that there are some things that we can change. Have a look at this and tell me what you think," she said.

I scanned the sheet and grimaced. I was never one for budgeting and I certainly didn't like being told that I would have to cut back on my spending. The mobile phone plan was an important one and I felt sure that I would find a way to persuade Kay why I should keep it. I put the sheet down and proceeded to carry on with my other tasks at hand.

A couple of days later, Kay came back with another budget. "I've been reviewing things and maybe you will need to cut back on your coffees and bought lunches. You can take a sandwich into work instead," she announced as budget version 2.0 was introduced.

And so it carried on. Every few days Kay would announce yet another iteration of the budget and show innovative ways that we could make ends meet. By the time she introduced version 23 (okay, I might be exaggerating this number), I listened to her and then asked her the following question, "And what do you think that you are telling God by producing all these versions of your budgets?"

"I guess that I'm telling Him that I don't trust Him?" Kay considerately replied.

"Exactly! Maybe you should rely on Him more and allow Him to provide." I said. "After all, the Bible tells us that God 'knows every hair on your head and provides for every need of the sparrow'. I'm sure that He could provide for us."

Kay never needed to provide another household budget after that point.

Six months later, on the 8th of May, Kay and I clutched our towels as we stood by the baptismal pool on the stage at Church. We had made another step in faith to follow the instructions to walk in the footsteps of Jesus and become water baptized.

In effect, we were saying goodbye to our old selves by full immersion in the waters and coming up clean and washed of sin – emerging as the 'new man' in Christ. Full of faith and new hope, we entered the waters as sinners and emerged as victors, changed by the grace of God and the sacrifice of His Son and the shedding of His blood for our sins on the cross.

When I emerged out of the waters, I received a vision from God that two years from that day, we would become debt-free. As I shared this promise with Kay, we jumped with joy. Finally, something good was going to come out of all this faith.

Time doesn't wait for anybody. I immediately started to plan my financial freedom and for 18 months I struggled to make God's promise come to life.

I reasoned that if I grew my Amway business, and went Emerald, then Diamond, we would receive enough bonuses to become debt-free. But that wasn't it.

So, I focussed on my work, trying to add value to my clients. Maybe that would lead to extra bonuses and promotions that would help us become debt-free. But that proved to be yet another dead end that I would have to reverse out of.

With help from Paul Adams, who happened to be a Realtor as well as an elder at Church, I thought that I could fast-track my way to financial freedom by selling my dream house and downsizing it. Until Kay saw the shoe-box of a home that we would have to cram ourselves into and she screamed, "No way!!!" to this hare-brained idea of mine.

Then I finally figured it out... I was going to win the Readers Digest Prize Draw!!

I'm sure that you can see the irony of me telling Kay to have faith in God providing for us. Yet, ironically, this was lost on me. Where was my faith? I was purely carnal, wanting to do it all in my strength. As humorous as it sounded, none of these ideas made sense nor did any work out. And it was with frustrated indignation that I finally gave up on the notion of getting us debt-free.

Fast forward a few years... It was January 2007. I was relieved to touchdown back onto New Zealand soil. Our holiday to Greece and Australia had turned into more of a nightmare than the relaxing time that we had planned. The spiritual attacks seemed to escalate during that period.

Two days after we arrived at my parent's apartment in Greece, our daughter broke out into the worst case of chickenpox that any of us had observed. Then our son, who had scraped his ankle a few days prior to leaving New Zealand, required an intensive course of antibiotics to treat his wound that had turned septic.

Living in a cramped apartment, we were joined by my niece and nephew who were visiting family over Christmas. Unbeknown to me, my niece had contracted strep-throat which in turn was passed on to Kay and me, making it difficult for either of us to swallow, let alone eat, for nearly 4 days.

Averaging as little as two hours of uninterrupted sleep during this period, the strain was beginning to show on me.

Our children, then aged five and four, were under strict instructions to minimize the noise they made during the day, especially between 1 - 4 pm when the majority of the locals took their siestas. To add to our misery, the apartment was located across the road from the local football stadium and less than 100 meters from the local church, which rang its bells regularly and as early as 6am!

Soon I was counting down the days to our departure from Greece to Australia, where we were looking forward to chilling out with our good friends in Perth.

Just as I thought that things couldn't get any worse, my son broke out with chickenpox that was so extreme that it made his sister's case look like a minor irritation from a mosquito bite. Alarmed at the sight of his grandson's red blotchy face, my father called in the doctor for a house visit.

"This looks bad," the doctor confirmed in her heavily accented English. "It impossible for him to travel, specifically if there are elderly passengers on the plane. You have no choice - postpone your departure."

This wasn't the news that either Kay or I wanted to hear. Reluctantly we took the note written by the doctor to the Emirates office and postponed our departure by 3 days, delaying the respite that we would get. This was the straw that broke the camel's back.

Kay and I vowed that things would have to change by the time we returned home, and four days later, when we arrived in Perth, we started to plan a new course of action that would lead us to a better and more fulfilled life.

Kay committed to restarting her undergraduate studies and I committed to securing a new role.

Kay had started a part-time role at Church, having volunteered her time over the previous year with the newly established school. Her dedication and attention to detail had made a positive impact on a Pastor, who recommended her for employment within the Church.

Whilst the hours were limited to 24 per week, the income was welcome. It was still well below Kay's previous income level, but it offered her a sense of recognition that she needed and deserved.

As we reviewed our bank account, we realized that we were still going backward. Our overall debt was sitting over $160,000 and we were only able to make the minimum payments on our credit card. I started to doubt that God's promise of financial freedom that He gave us would ever come to fruition. But I held on to the promise that His word never came back void.

Towards the end of January, the Church kicked off the New Year with a Leadership Weekend. The theme that year was "Paint the Town Red." It was all related to going out into the community and performing random acts of Christian kindness.

Sitting in the congregation, enjoying the praise and worship, I started to thank God for the blessings that I had received in my life. With my arms raised in praise, I was reflecting about the wonders of God and the miracles that He could deliver. With a sense of surrender, I heard God speak to me.

"Give Me your burden and take on Mine," the Lord told me.

"Sure, I'll give you my burden," I replied. "I want to become debt-free. I'll give You THAT burden, God. After all, that was YOUR idea! I've tried everything that I could to become debt-free, but it hasn't worked out. Good luck. I hope that YOU can do it! Now tell me, what burden do You want me to take on?"

"Be salt and light," was all that God said.

"Give me a break – what's THAT supposed to mean?" I enquired.

And God defined His burden through the scripture in Matthew 25:31-46, which He summarised to me with the following phrase,

> "When I was hungry, you fed me, when I was naked, you clothed me, when I was in prison, you visited me..."

"Yep, I can do that," I replied. And with that, I took on my commission from God.

TIME TO REFLECT...

What are some of the learning lessons in this experience?

Keep your eye on the big picture.

When God makes a promise, it will come to pass.

You have to have faith that He will provide.

You need to step aside and let Him take charge of the steering wheel.

If you can become His hands and feet, He will reward you.

And you can't underestimate the faith that your spouse has when it compares to yours!

CHAPTER FOURTEEN

Why bother painting the town red?

I returned to Church later on that afternoon. In keeping with the theme of painting the town red, I understood that we would be praying and evangelizing across town. And this was going to take me well outside of my comfort zone.

As I pulled my car into the busy car park, I scanned the landscape until I found a space big enough to slip my car into.

I only knew a handful of people within the Church, and most of them were acquaintances that I had met through the Gateway course. Walking towards the main entrance of the Church, I realized that many people had already been allocated tasks and had headed out. Only a handful of people milled around.

City Impact Church is known as a mega-church in New Zealand and in 2007 boasted a congregation in the region of 2,000 people. With an auditorium capable of seating 800 - 900 people, we were already accustomed to running two daytime services. So it wasn't unusual not to know or be known to the other members of the congregation.

As I approached one of the Pastors, I was simply seeking direction. In front of him was a minivan, full of its quota of passengers. The Pastor eyed me up and then turned around to one of the occupants in the minivan. "Come on, my little friend," the Pastor casually commented. "Make way for this fella to take your place."

As the young boy exited the vehicle and I took his place, I was introduced to the vehicle owners, Steve and Jalaine, and a lovely couple from the South Island campus, Shaun and his heavily pregnant wife Vanessa. I was told that our assignment was to pray over the campus of the University of Auckland.

I had never undertaken such a bold task as this before. I was nervously apprehensive as we made our way into town. Sitting in the back of the minivan by myself, I contributed sparingly to the conversation. The instructions were read out for all to hear.

We were told to pray publicly within the vicinity we were allocated and then to continue into town, where we were encouraged to perform some random acts of Christian kindness. To help stimulate our creative juices, some examples were listed. Offer to buy somebody a meal; help somebody to move some furniture; talk to an elderly person...

Before I knew it, I felt the car come to a halt as we parked across the road from the university campus. I was the last to exit the vehicle and decided to follow the lead of the others. They walked around the campus and stood outside the doors to one of the main entrances.

"Well I guess there's nothing like the present," said Steve. "Let's spread around and start praying!"

Soon we walked off in different directions and I heard the heavenly languages being prayed by my companions start to fade into whispers as the distances between us all increased. Self-conscious at first, I mumbled some prayers under my breath, scanning around for potential intruders who might embarrass me and catch me out in my task.

As I continued to walk around uninterrupted by passers-by, I grew in courage and started to pray boldly in my recently acquired heavenly language. My steps took meaning and soon I was striding around with confidence and purpose. Within a relatively short amount of time, I had lost many of my inhibitions as I allowed the Holy Spirit to guide me and my purposeful prayer.

Within the blink of an eye, we regrouped as our allocated 30 minutes of prayer time had expired. Euphoric from our exertions, we headed down the hill and made our way towards the central business district and Queen Street. Full of adrenalin, we shared ideas on how we could bless people. We stopped random strangers that passed by us, paid them compliments and proceeded to hand out flyers inviting them to a Church service.

Queen Street started to loom in front of us and we noticed the flashing lights that beckoned weary visitors into the comfort of the budget backpackers ahead on our right.

"We should go in there and bless someone," Shaun suggested out loud, and with a happy roar of united agreement, we all turned as one into the backpackers.

"How much does it cost for a night's accommodation?" Steve enquired of the clerk behind the counter.

"You want a room for the night?" he replied.

"Nope, I just want to know how much it costs to spend a night here," Steve clarified.

"It's $20 per night," the clerk confirmed.

"Great! Here's $20 which we would like to put towards the cost of the next person that comes in looking for a room tonight." And between Steve and Shaun, they handed over the required tariff.

"But why do you want to do that," the curious clerk asked them.

"Because," they said, handing over a Church flyer, "we want to bless them! We're from City Impact Church and we'd like you to let them know that we have already pre-paid for their stay. Please give them one of these flyers so that they know who we are!" And just as quickly, we exited the backpackers and continued towards Queen Street.

I was impressed by how simple this task was. Whilst I waited for the lights to change and give us safe passage to the other side of Queen Street, I noticed a large crowd gathered outside of the Civic Theatre, awaiting entry to watch their play. Jalaine and Vanessa decided to pop into the local dairy and purchase lollies that they could distribute to the expectant crowd.

As I waited for them outside the dairy, I thought to myself, "What can I do?"

And no sooner had I thought the question than I heard a still, quiet voice inside my head say, "How much money do you have in your wallet?" (I would later come to recognize this voice as the Holy Spirit.)

I pulled out my wallet and saw that I only had $10 on me. "Give that to the next taxi driver and ask him to put it towards his next fare," the voice instructed.

I continued to walk along Queen Street and past the crowd and headed towards Aotea Square, scanning the road for a taxi. Who could believe that there were no taxis on Queen Street on a Saturday evening! This was unheard of.

In the distance, I spotted a taxi cruising down the road from Upper Queen Street. It slowed down as it got closer and suddenly it stopped beside me. I opened the front door and bent down to speak to the driver.

"I don't need a lift, but I wanted to give you this money so that you might be able to bless the next passenger that you pick up," I explained. "I'd like to bless them, on behalf of City Impact Church!"

"Oh, that is a real blessings," the taxi driver said in his heavily accented English. "Don't you knows how much this helps..."

I recognized the accent and determined that the driver was of Arabic descent.

"Inta min whayn?" I said in Arabic.

"Anna Mussri!" the taxi driver exclaimed in surprise! "I'm from Jordan! Are you Arab?"

"No, I'm a Greek," I explained. "I was born in Libya and I understand and speak a little Arabic!"

"I'm political refugee," the taxi driver continued. He lifted up his shirt and showed me a scar that covered a third of his lower stomach. "They shooted me. Trys to kills me, but kills my uncle!"

After a short dialogue, we exchanged phone numbers and I waved the taxi driver away. Suddenly I felt 10 feet tall and bulletproof! Buoyed on by this newly found confidence, I followed my colleagues, entered Aotea Square and started to speak to the various stallholders. In front of me stood a man dismantling his stand.

"How's it going?" I enquired as I started some small talk.

I soon found out that the man I was talking to had not had the best of days, and that he was battling some challenging times.

"I'm a man of faith," I went on to explain. "Would you mind if my friends and I pray for you?"

With the consented approval from this man, I proceeded to pray for him and call the powers of Heaven down to Earth for his benefit. And suddenly, I realized that taking on God's burden was actually a lot less onerous than I had at first anticipated!

The following week I received a call from the taxi driver. He wanted to thank me for my generous gesture and invited me over for a coffee at his apartment.

With the date agreed upon, I ventured over at the appointed time. The apartment was located in a small apartment block in Kingsland. Parking outside the building was at a premium, but I managed to find a spot to reverse my car into.

An intercom system controlled the privacy that separated the taxi driver from the outside world. The sound of the buzzing electronics indicated that the gate had been released and I opened it and slipped over to the other side. I navigated the course prescribed by the taxi driver and soon found myself outside the open door of an apartment on the third floor.

I was ushered in with all the usual generous and hospitable welcome associated with the Middle Eastern culture. Various snacks were already prepared and laid out on the table. Baklava, Turkish Delights, and pistachio nuts adorned the table alongside dips that I was familiar with.

The taxi driver offered me a coffee which I expected and gratefully accepted. But the conversation with the taxi driver did not adhere to the standard script that I was anticipating.

During the 90 minutes we were together, the taxi driver started to share his story and the testimony of how I became an answer to his prayer.

It turned out that he was a Christian who had been living in the predominantly Muslim kingdom of Jordan. He was a vocal and active man, often seen on TV or heard on radio advocating the love of Jesus Christ and talking about the truth of His word. Unfortunately, this message wasn't well-received by the Muslim extremists in the region.

Soon there was a bounty placed upon the taxi driver's head and a reward was offered for his death.

He was used to living under the shadow of death as many others before him had been picked off in the region. But a sensible lifestyle and outward diligence was sufficient to keep him and others alive.

One day, when he was out walking with his uncle, a car screeched to a halt in the road beside them and three men rushed out and gunned them down in broad daylight with their Kalashnikovs. Both the taxi driver and his uncle instantaneously fell to the ground and their blood mingled on the pavement and stained the concrete slabs that they lay lifeless on.

The taxi driver went on to say that he had been badly wounded and many feared that he had instantaneously died during the attack. Bullets had ripped through his intestine and his blood loss was profuse. His uncle died at the scene, but due to some miracle, the taxi driver managed to survive long enough to be transported to the hospital, where the surgical team operated on him.

After eight hours of intensive surgery and many liters of blood transfusions, his life was spared and he made a slow, but eventual recovery. Living in Jordan became untenable and he soon applied for emigration to New Zealand where he was granted entry as a political refugee.

His integration into the New Zealand culture was facilitated with the aid of a job as a taxi driver and supplemented with a small welfare aid. He went on to explain that the previous Saturday night, he sat in his apartment, without two pennies to rub together. He was desperate as his car had no petrol and he had no money to pay for any.

Searching for a solution, the taxi driver explained that he dropped to his knees and prayed to God for an answer to his dilemma, God responded by telling him to get into his car and drive it down to Queen Street, where a solution would appear.

"But I don't have enough petrol to drive that far," the taxi driver argued with God.

"Do it anyway," was God's direct answer.

And with faith as big as a mustard seed, he started his engine and made the short trip down to Queen Street. Since the majority of the journey was downhill, he even switched his engine off and just allowed his car to cruise down the road, letting gravity carry him along and preserve the fumes that constituted what little fuel that remained.

By the time he met me, he was unsure that he would even have enough petrol to allow him to drive back home, let alone take a fare to their destination. Yet the blessing of the $10 was enough to enable him to fill up with a little petrol and carry on for the night.

It would turn out that his takings that evening were the highest he had ever achieved since he started driving taxis. And he wanted to let me know that my generosity had led to his good fortune.

As I left the apartment and jumped into my car, I felt goose-bumps on my arms. I had a revelation about the power of the God that I serve. My obedience to listen to the still, small voice in my head ended up having a tremendous impact on another person's life.

I felt inspired, knowing that we could hear God give specific instructions that could lead to a blessing somewhere. Even though the taxi driver was the person who benefited from my actions, it was I who now felt blessed, knowing that my seemingly inconsequential action had a massive impact.

"How do you get debt-free?" This is a question that I am often asked. To help answer this, let me share with you how God helped us to get debt-free the first time.

Having made the decision that I was going to look for a new job, I became inundated with five different opportunities. Soon they whittled down to one. I had been interviewed for a role at Vodafone and throughout the interview process, I was reassured that the role was mine. It reached a point that I had received a verbal offer, and just needed to get the written confirmation in place.

I was desperate to move on. I had even printed a copy of my resignation letter, which just needed dating and my signature to make it official. If I had it my way, I would have dated and signed it the day that I received the verbal offer. However, Kay forbade me from doing that. Under no circumstances was I allowed to hand it in until I had the written offer in my hand! It seemed to take ages for the written offer to materialize. Soon the clock ticked over three months from the verbal offer. And still nothing! I wondered if this offer was real or not.

We arrived at church early on Sunday morning. I had just completed another fast and was praying for the breakthrough in relation to receiving this written job offer.

As I paused to sip my coffee prior to the start of the service, I looked across at Kay. "I've been thinking about my situation," I announced. "I have been waiting patiently for this breakthrough with Vodafone. So far, I've been praying and fasting, but sometimes I feel that I haven't made all the breakthroughs that God is asking for. I think that there's one more thing for me to step out in faith."

Our Church was taking up a sacrificial offering and this was the appointed day. I went on to explain that I had been praying about our offering and I had received a revelation about it.

"In scripture, it says in Luke 6:38 'Give, and it will be given to you: good measure, pressed down, shaken together, and running over will be put into your bosom. For with the same measure that you use, it will be measured back to you'." With that out in the open, I went on to explain that I felt God encouraging me to put a particular amount into the sacrificial offering that day. Kay was a little taken aback when she heard the amount.

That day we held hands as we walked up to the front of the Church and deposited our envelope with our sacrificial offering in front of the altar to God.

In the week that followed the sacrificial offering, the day finally arrived when I received a call to tell me that a written offer was available for me to counter-sign.

I pocketed my cellphone and walked out of the office and took the lift from the 19th floor to the lobby. I exited the building and turned left, continuing down Hobson Street towards the Viaduct and to the recruitment consultant's office.

In front of me were two copies of the letter of employment, which I was asked to read through and then sign. As I read the document, I observed the remuneration plan and understood that the promise of God was about to be birthed. The values exceeded my expectations. I took pleasure in signing both copies of the contract and warmly shook the recruitment consultant's hand as I departed his office, with my personalised 'debt-reduction gun' in my hand.

I was looking forward to using it to apply against my debt and help to reduce it to a mere speck.

I had more of a bounce in my step as I walked back to the office, entered the lobby and called the lift that would usher me back up to the 19th floor. As I got out of the lift, the smile that creased my face and threatened to split it in half announced my intentions to my colleagues even before I had the chance to say anything.

I walked to my desk, took out my resignation letter that was patiently awaiting my signature and its own birthdate to give it life. I completed the letter and placed it in an envelope and walked down the hall to my boss's office. "Sorry to bother you," I said, clearing my throat. "I just need to have a quick word. Do you have a minute now?"

With a resigned nod of my boss's head, I handed over the envelope and confirmed that I was officially handing in my notice.

"Any chance that we can get you to change your mind?" he asked me, more out of hope than conviction.

"Nope, sorry mate, my mind's made up!"

With the formalities over, I offered to complete certain tasks that would take me about 4 or 5 working days. My plan was accepted, and I was advised to take the rest of my months' notice as garden leave, which was ideal for me. With a shake of hands, I did a U-turn and left the office.

I walked back into my office and my colleagues turned in their seats and asked the inevitable question, "How did he take it?"

"He was great," I replied. "We have agreed that I will complete the work outstanding on a few accounts and prepare handover material which will take me through to next Wednesday. I can do that from home and then I'll be on garden leave until next month. So I'll head off home now – you can get hold of me on my cellphone – and I'll see you for drinks in a month's time!"

I picked up my personal belongings and for the penultimate time, left the office and headed home.

I pulled out the calculator from the drawer next to Kay's desk at home. I punched the keys and looked up at her. To my amazement, the increase in my salary was equal to 10 times our sacrificial offering! I shared the news with Kay and beamed in admiration of God's power.

On Sunday I wrote a praise report, which was passed over to the Senior Pastor alongside the prayer requests.

After the praise and worship, my praise report was read out by Pastor Peter. "Elias Kanaris has written a praise report that I'd like to read out. 'A few weeks ago we had the sacrificial offering. After praying and fasting I gave a certain amount that was quite a stretch for us. It was made in relation to a new job offer I was waiting on. This week I received the offer and the increase in salary was exactly 10 times my offering.' Maybe you should have given more, and you would have received an even bigger pay increase!" he concluded. And on that note, I joined the congregation in a hearty laugh.

TIME TO REFLECT...

What are some of the learning lessons in this experience?

God will multiply your seed. Sometimes it is 10-fold, sometimes it is 30-fold and sometimes it is 60-fold.

A sacrificial offering is exactly that, a sacrifice. It took a big step of faith to place that big an offering, but the reward was 10-fold.

I often hear praise reports after a sacrificial offering that points to God's favor over people's lives.

CHAPTER FIFTEEN

What are the unexpected benefits of leaving one job for another?

Once I tidied up the loose ends at work, I headed straight into the building work at our Church. It was a match made in heaven. We were in the middle of a major extension to our facility, building a state-of-the-art sanctuary that could seat up to 2,000.

I took the opportunity to spend time on-site, helping out wherever I was required. For part of the time, I was involved with digging drains, at other times with setting up the framing for the new concrete staircase. Irrespective of the role, I was super excited about the opportunity.

I would often return home dirty and tired but satisfied that I was like Nehemiah, taking on the building project to rebuild the walls of God's sanctuary.

Soon the days passed by and I neared my last day at work.

I finished my shift on the building site at lunchtime and headed home, where I showered and got ready for my final drinks with my soon-to-be ex-colleagues. As agreed, I visited the office on my way to the pub and checked in with the office administrator.

They finalized the paperwork and I handed over my carpark permit and the access card as I signed off from one chapter of my career. Together, we reviewed my HR record.

"It would appear that you have just over four days of annual leave registered in the system," the administrator mentioned as she pointed me to the information on her screen. "Does that seem right to you?"

"Yes, it does," I replied.

With little fanfare, we completed our administrative tasks and concluded the formalities. I thanked her and caught up with my colleagues in the hall. "It looks like beer-o'clock!" they said happily and trundled in the lift to start our short journey across the road to the pub.

As was the policy at the time, drinks were to be supplied and paid for by the individuals and not the company. I opened the party by buying drinks all round and asked for the first platter of food to be delivered.

Soon the room became crowded as more people joined in the festivities as their various tasks concluded and they entered their weekend celebration via the pub. The mood was chipper, and the atmosphere was jovial. Old war stories were shared, and laughter penetrated the room.

Out of the corner of my eye, I noticed my colleague, Rachel, enter the room. She was already six months pregnant and rosy-cheeked. She came up to me, breathless with excitement and gave me a friendly hug and offered me hearty congratulations.

"Is that for joining the enemy or managing to escape from here?" I asked her.

Rachel had shared an office with me and two other colleagues. She worked for the finance team and had participated in a number of projects involved with the restructure of the organization following yet another merger.

"I'm excited for you," she said. "They finally approved that everyone working for the company as of today will qualify for a guaranteed 90% of their bonuses. Congratulations!"

I chuckled as I heard the news. "That sounds great, Rachel, but it wouldn't affect me. Number one, today is my last day here. I've already resigned and I'm heading out of the door right now! Number two, I'm joining the competition. Why would they want to reward somebody joining the 'dark side'? And

WHAT ARE THE UNEXPECTED BENEFITS OF LEAVING ONE JOB FOR ANOTHER?

number three, I have nothing that I can claim against."

"Trust me," Rachel went on to say, "It has been approved. I should know, I was there in the room!"

The comment piqued my interest, but I didn't dwell on the topic for any length of time. "I'll believe that when I see it!"

A shove in my back almost made me spill my orange juice all over Rachel and I turned around to see which clumsy person had potentially exceeded their quota of alcohol for the evening. With a shout of joy, colleagues from the previous department I worked in converged around me and gave me a group hug. Soon the topic of conversation with Rachel was forgotten as laughter once again crossed the room, with jokes and memories becoming the mixers and tonics required to wash away the stress of another week in the office.

By 8:30 pm the crowd in the room had thinned out and I found myself surrounded by a handful of close friends. Happy and satisfied that some food was still available for them to soak up their alcoholic intake, I wished them a fond farewell and picked up my going away presents and card and headed back out to the car.

The cloudless sky and empty roads made the journey home pleasant and I parked my car in the garage before heading upstairs to tuck the kids in bed and say prayers with them.

I then sat down with Kay and shared some of the highlights with her.

"You'll never guess what Rachel said... she reckons that they will pay up 90% of my bonuses year-to-date. No questions asked!"

"Bonuses paid – Yeah, right," Kay replied. "That sounds like another Tui's billboard ad coming up!"

The next day I woke up with a sense of anticipation. What if Rachel had been correct?

As I lay in bed, I started praying to God, thanking Him for everything that He had done for me and my family. I thanked Him for the great group of friends that I was leaving behind at work and lifted many of them in prayer by name, for success in their work as well as their personal relationships and health.

With Kay still asleep beside me, I quietly slipped out of bed and headed out of the bedroom, shutting the door behind me. I saw the kids sitting in front of the TV in the lounge and went up to them and gave them a massive hug before preparing some breakfast.

With my duties completed, I made myself a coffee and headed downstairs to my office to check up on emails.

I shook my mouse to wake the screen up and waited for the few moments between action and reaction as the screen lazily came to life. With my browser opened, I clicked on the bookmarks before selecting my on-line bank. I entered my account id and password and took a sip from my coffee whilst I waited for the screen to refresh.

To my surprise, the account balances on the main screen didn't seem quite right. I leaned into the screen and took another look.

With a click of the mouse, I started a deeper dive at the data behind my inflated bank balance and I became impatient for the screen to refresh. My heart starting beating faster and I felt the anticipation of my miracle commencing to unfold in front of me.

Sure enough, there was a deposit made by my ex-employer for an unusually high sum of money. "Well blow me down!" I thought. "Rachel was right after all!"

I chuckled to myself as here was the five-figure deposit despite my suspicions.

As soon as I logged out of my account, I opened up my emails and saw one from my ex-employer. But the email told a different story than the one I was expecting to hear.

I opened the attachment and started reviewing the information. I noticed that the final payment was not made up of a combination of base pay and bonuses as Rachel had led me to believe. It was made up of base pay and a LOT of holiday pay. As I analyzed the payslip in more detail, it became apparent that there were mysterious forces at play here.

According to the documentation provided, I had received an additional 30+ days of holiday pay on top of the allocated holiday pay that I was expecting. I could not get my head around this anomaly. I had checked the online

WHAT ARE THE UNEXPECTED BENEFITS OF LEAVING ONE JOB FOR ANOTHER?

system at work the previous day and what I remember seeing was that I had accumulated less than five days of holiday leave entitlement. (A few days later I would find out that this wasn't a mistake, but the entitlement that they had in their system. To this day, I cannot explain how this happened, except to put it down as a mircle!)

I raised my head towards heaven and gave God a mighty shout of joy! This could only have been His doing.

With a happy smirk on my face, I walked back upstairs and gently opened my bedroom door. I saw Kay propped up on her pillows reading a book.

"You'll never guess what happened," I said to Kay.

"You got paid your bonus?" she asked, excitedly.

"No, even more bizarre than that," I replied. "I got paid an additional 30+ days of holiday allowance that I was sure I didn't qualify for. There's tens of thousands of dollars sitting in the account. Praise The Lord for His generosity!"

"Praise The Lord indeed," Kay agreed.

"I'd better tell Rachel that she was wrong," I said as I gave Kay a high-five and then hugged and kissed her before leaving the room.

With my cellphone in my hand, I sent Rachel a simple text. It read:

'Sorry Rachel, you were wrong! No bonus payments made in my final pay. I knew that it was too good to believe! LOL Have a gr8 weekend. Cheers EK'.

I put down my phone and finished my coffee before getting changed to go back to Church and work with my fellow congregants on the sanctuary build again.

As I drove through the Church gates, my cellphone announced an incoming text. I waited until I parked my car and checked the text out. It was a reply from Rachel. All it said was: 'No dummy, bonuses are paid in alternative pay cycle. Check again in 2 weeks... Rachel'.

The next two weeks sped by as I stepped into my new role at Vodafone. The open plan environment was somewhat unusual and took a little getting used to. With no assigned seating, the work environment was much less structured than I was used to, as well as being more informal.

Because I had joined in the middle of what was known in the industry as a 'brown-out period', they were unable to get my new phone connected to the network, so I had to rely on my personal cellphone in the interim period.

Soon I was mingling with people that I last worked with 12 years earlier when I had secured my first role in New Zealand. In addition, the smaller workforce meant that I was soon well known within the company.

As my working day ground to a halt during the latter half of the week, I received a call that I answered. "Good afternoon, you're through to Elias Kanaris."

"Hello there, I was trying to get hold of Patricia, is she there?"

As I listened to the female voice, I was trying to figure out why I had received this wrong number. "I'm sorry; you might have dialed the wrong number. Who were you after?"

"Patricia Kanaris," said the caller. "We had this number registered against her account."

"Oh, you're after my wife! Sorry about that, hardly anyone calls her by her first name. You're through to her husband. You'll need to try her on the following number..." I detailed the correct number to the caller and asked one final question. "If you can tell me who's calling, I'll make sure that she knows and gets back to you as soon as possible."

"Most certainly," the caller obliged. "Can you tell her that it is Consumer Magazine calling?"

After I hung up the phone, I got on with my work after I sent Kay a text letting her know that she should expect a call from Consumer Magazine. Within five minutes my afternoon was interrupted again as my cellphone rang for the second time. This time it was Kay calling.

"You'll never guess what just happened to me," she said. "I just got a call from Consumer Magazine. Remember the letter that I sent through to them a few months back, asking for their advice on the refund note that the store wouldn't honor. Well, as you know, my letter was published as the letter of the month and as a result, I received a free annual subscription this year."

I nodded my head in agreement, grunting a response back to Kay.

"Well, it turns out that they do an annual draw amongst their subscribers and they pulled MY name out of a hat and I just won a laptop!" We both burst

WHAT ARE THE UNEXPECTED BENEFITS OF LEAVING ONE JOB FOR ANOTHER?

into laughter as the news sunk in. Was there no limit to the blessings that we would receive from God?

By the end of the second week, I was slowly getting used to my new work environment. It was much more relaxed than my last job and I had the freedom to come and go as I pleased. The open plan environment extended down to the car park, where they had valet parking in place.

As I arrived at work, I would let the staff know the approximate time of departure and they would double or triple park my car in the depths of the building. With a valet parking ticket in my hand, I only had to text them the number 10 to 15 minutes before I was due to leave and they would ensure that my car was ready for me to drive off.

I decided to leave work just after 2 pm on that Friday and worked my way back home from the Viaduct. The traffic was light and I cruised through to Constellation Drive, where I exited the motorway and headed home.

I dropped off a few items at home and carried on to Church where I picked up the kids from school. Soon we were back at home getting ready to settle in for the weekend. By 4:30 pm Kay had finished up at work and was at home by my side.

After dinner, we sat in the lounge and watched TV together, playing a DVD that the kids had chosen. Soon our evening routine reached the point that the kids were once again tucked into bed, and prayers were said before the lights were turned out.

I followed Kay downstairs and we settled into our routine of checking emails and surfing the net.

As was my habit, I logged into the bank account to make sure that there was enough money there to pay the fortnightly installment for the mortgage. A smile creased my face as there, by divine decree, was another lump sum payment from my previous employer, as predicted by Rachel. I was starting to realise that this was not luck, but favor from God!

"Guess what I found," I teased Kay. "A lump sum payment from my old employer. You beauty!"

The five-figure sum of money was a sight for sore eyes and once again, Kay and I gave thanks to the glory of God and His abundant blessings. At this rate, it would take us less than a year to clear that debt. All we needed to do was to be frugal with our pay and ensure that every penny went on retiring the debt that we had.

Every penny, that is, that was left over after the 10% that we automatically tithed to Church.

I smiled as I thought through the futile attempts that I had made to get myself and my family debt-free. Yet this five-figure bonus payment became an iconic representation of God's power and capability. This time I made sure that I sent Rachel a text expressing my pleasure at the outcome!

Ironically, a month later I received yet another bonus payment from my ex-employer. Admittedly it was about a tenth of the value of the previous bonus payment. Maybe, I thought to myself, I should let them know that I have left. When I checked with Rachel she reminded me that bonus payments were always made in arrears. This would be the last payment that I received!

It didn't take us a year to get debt-free. About a month later my mum called me from Athens. She wanted to know how we were getting on in our new house. I gave her a run-down of the work that we had completed after we moved in. She was also curious to know how my new job was going. I took great pleasure in letting her know.

It was before she had a computer or an email account. We only communicated via phone calls or via the dreadfully slow snail-mail.

As we talked, she asked me whether we had a loan on the house. I confirmed that we did. She pressed me for further details, including the amount that we owed. I told her what was left outstanding on the mortgage.

Due to the bonus payments and the unexpected extra holiday pay, we had managed to significantly reduce our debt. With our more frugal lifestyle, by allocating every penny towards the mortgage, and Kay's weekly paycheque, we were down to about $100,000.

"That's not right," my mum said. "I'll talk to your dad. I don't think that

WHAT ARE THE UNEXPECTED BENEFITS OF LEAVING ONE JOB FOR ANOTHER?

you should be paying any interest."

I tried to talk my mum out of this hair-brained idea of hers. Her parting words on the call was, "Leave it with me!"

The following day she called me out of the blue. Normally it would be a week or two between calls. I was concerned that something bad had happened to her or dad. To my surprise, she was the bearer of great tidings. My dad had agreed to cover the balance of our mortgage.

Within a week the paperwork was processed, and the money was wired over to us.

Almost two years from the day of our water baptism, we found ourselves debt-free! Some of you will be reading this and saying that it was just a lucky break. I say that it was God blessing us...

TIME TO REFLECT...

What are some of the learning lessons in this experience?

When God makes a promise, it comes true.

You don't have to understand the 'how'.

The closer you get to God the easier that it becomes.

LEVERAGING GOD

CHAPTER SIXTEEN

What would you do if you woke up and found yourself $2,000,000 in debt?

―――――

We were blessed. After the 2008 general election finished, I made the decision not to return to the corporate world. Instead, I ventured out into my own business. With hindsight, you need to ask the question, "Was 2009 the best time to start a business?"

2008 heralded the GFC (Global Financial Crisis). This was our modern-day equivalent of the Great Depression!

Here is a definition that the internet throws up to help us define the GFC:

> "The financial crisis was primarily caused by deregulation in the financial industry. That permitted banks to engage in hedge fund trading with derivatives... When the values of the derivatives crumbled, banks stopped lending to each other. That created the financial crisis that led to the Great Recession." (Ref:https://www.thebalance.com/what-caused-2008-global-financial-crisis-3306176)

Now, I don't know about you, but I needed someone to break this down into something that I could understand and get my teeth into...

Maybe you have heard about the term 'subprime mortgage'. Let's start there.

A subprime loan is a loan that has interest rates that are higher than the prime rate. Subprime borrowers generally tend to be individuals who have low credit ratings, or maybe even a person who was perceived of as likely to default on a loan. Overall, the people who would apply for subprime loans were individuals who, on the whole, would not qualify for conventional mortgages.

Interestingly enough, the term 'subprime' refers to the borrower and their financial situation rather than the loan itself. Either way, when you research the term, it contains one common word: "risk".

A majority of the loans were issued as interest-only loans, at an interest rate that was already above the prime rate. Property valuations became inflated and this created an asset bubble in the real estate market that eventually exploded in 2008. The people who borrowed these interest-only loans often purchased their properties for 100% mortgages (or at best a very small deposit).

When the initial interest-free period expired, the borrower was either forced into a principal and interest payment or pushed to an even higher interest rate. Many could not afford their repayments and started to default.

The value of their properties were inflated and efforts to sell their properties proved fruitless. For many, their assets had reduced in value.

Unfortunately, the market overcompensated with a number of subprime loans defaulting, causing financial ripples that crippled the world economically.

Here in New Zealand, the ripple took longer to reach us. The effects were felt in 2009 when the banks started to tighten up their lending criteria. Obtaining a loan was a rarity.

Let's set the scene. I found myself debt-free, with no job and a new business that had no track record. The key here is in the phrase, "I found myself debt-free".

WHAT WOULD YOU DO IF YOU WOKE UP AND FOUND YOURSELF $2,000,000 IN DEBT?

I was the classic asset-rich, cash-poor person that author and speaker Robert Kiyosaki writes about in his book, "Rich Dad, Poor Dad".

Rich Dad, Poor Dad is about Robert Kiyosaki and his two dads – his real father (poor dad) and the father of his best friend (rich dad) – and the ways in which both men shaped his thoughts about money and investing. You don't need to earn a high income to be rich. Rich people make money work for them.

So, when Paul Adams approached me in June 2009 with a property investment opportunity, I started to apply the principles of Rich Dad and put my assets to work.

The home that we had purchased in 2005 had appreciated in value. According to the bank, we had enough equity to qualify for a 100% loan on the purchase of this second property. If you looked at our situation, we were defying all the odds.

But our blessing didn't stop there. Soon we were offered a second property and then a third.

With each property, we approached the bank and they advanced us 100% loans on each property and gave them to us as interest-only loans. Were we becoming a subprime borrower here in New Zealand?

Life was rosy. We had tenants that provided enough income to cover more than 90% of our interest payments. The balance of the payments required to cover the interest, local taxes (known as 'rates') and insurance was a form of enforced 'savings scheme'. We knew that eventually the properties would appreciate in value and we would recognize the gain when we sold the properties.

Thankfully, at the time of writing this book, we are still one of the privileged countries in the western world that don't have capital gains tax. Whatever we made, we would keep.

When we needed to release some equity, we sold a property. It was as simple as that.

Sure, we had to pay the real estate fees, as well as the solicitors, but the overall gain balanced itself out.

Over a coffee, I remember talking to a very successful business person who attended our Church. I explained to her that Kay and I had a vision to own as many as 10 investment properties. We wanted to make them available for Christian families that were fresh immigrants to New Zealand. Offering low and affordable rents to enable these families to get established, we saw ourselves as the guardians to the disadvantaged.

As I explained our vision, the person sitting opposite me sipped her coffee. When she placed her cup down on its saucer, she looked up at me and said, "Elias, is this a business or a charity?"

"It's a business," I replied.

"Then treat it like a business," she confirmed. "Don't treat it as a Charity, or that's what it will become."

Her words were a wake-up call. She was stating the blindingly obvious to me. But it was something that I was unwilling, up until that point, to acknowledge.

She added one more piece of advice. "Avoid working with Christians. They often want something for nothing!"

Halfway through 2013, I was approached by a person who I knew was a Christian. He was a property developer and was working with his son out of their offices approximately 45 minutes drive south of Auckland.

They had a property investment opportunity that they wanted to put in front of Kay and me to consider.

They had seen a property that sat in the corner of a 4,000 square meter section. The property had two roads that serviced the section. This meant that it was possible to subdivide the section, creating five new titles. These could be sold off as land and building packages by the developers, who would buy the title off us.

By the time you took the development costs into consideration, we would have covered the costs of the project by selling off the original home on a smaller section of land together with four of the five new titles. This would leave us with one section, on which they would build a house for us. The out-

WHAT WOULD YOU DO IF YOU WOKE UP AND FOUND YOURSELF $2,000,000 IN DEBT?

come? We would own a new house with built-in equity.

As it was explained to us, this project would take between 6 – 9 months to complete. It was a slam-dunk!

We went out to visit the property and Kay and I saw the expanse of land that we could own.

Due to the nature of the project, we approached the bank and sought yet another loan to take on this project. We were asked for significantly more financial information and we had to provide valuations on our existing properties. Thankfully, with an improving real estate market in Auckland, our properties had benefited from increasing house prices, caused to some extent to the lack of stock in the market.

Either way, the bank agreed to our loan request. When we told the developers, they were surprised to hear that the loan was written in such a way that it gave us the flexibility and scope to manage the funds as we desired.

By the time the bank was ready to loan us the money, and we were ready to complete the sale and purchase agreements for the purchase of the property, it was December the 4th. We visited our solicitor and signed the first round of paperwork. The following day, we re-entered her office and signed the paperwork to settle on the property.

On the next day, I boarded a plane to fly to Canada to attend the conference that I spoke about in chapter 1...

What I hadn't realized is that from the 5th of December 2013, I was walking around with a target on my back. The enemy didn't want me to succeed. The fact that God gave me a word at the conclusion of the Summit ("Elias, it's time for you to take over the stage...") meant that I became fair game for the enemy to attack.

The project that was supposed to take 6 – 9 months, stretched out to nearly four years.

Delays in getting Council approval was one of the many excuses that we received. Soon we found ourselves shelling out money and hemorrhaging as the interest charges piled on. The resource management costs to connect utilities such as the power and telecommunications were in the tens-of-thousands of dollars. Earth movement equipment bills started to mount up and progress didn't seem to match up with the original Gantt charts that we reviewed.

The excuses escalated and soon we found out that our development partners were battling a cashflow crisis of their own. Independent projects that they were developing in other parts of Auckland were running behind schedule and over budget.

Soon the inevitable happened. It was something that we should have seen, but I deliberately chose to ignore it.

TIME TO REFLECT...

What are some of the learning lessons in this experience?

You can become complacent.

If it sounds too good to be true – it probably is.

It is worth doing some due diligence and seeking God's instruction.

We had not sought God and one of the best ways to do that is to pray and fast and you cannot beat prayer and fasting.

CHAPTER SEVENTEEN

What is the writing on the wall?

There is a fascinating story told in the Old Testament book of Daniel (Chapter 5) that talks of king Belshazzar hosting a party in his palace. A thousand of his nobles joined him and they drank wine together.

The king gave orders for someone to bring him the gold and silver goblets that his father, king Nebuchadnezzar, had taken from the temple in Jerusalem.

As they sat there drinking from those goblets, the fingers of a human hand appeared and wrote on the plaster of the wall. Unsurprisingly, this upset and frightened the king. So much so, that

> "...his legs became weak and his knees were knocking."
> (Daniel 5:6, NIV)

Despite the best efforts of the enchanters, astrologers, and diviners of the time, none could read the writing or tell the king what it meant. It wasn't until Daniel was called upon to interpret the message that all was revealed.

Often, it seems, you need to get an outsider to give you an explanation of what the writing on the wall says.

One Saturday, after we had purchased the property, Kay and I traveled to the section with the kids to look over the land that we now owned. With our developer walking alongside us, we were re-sold the vision of this project. When the tour was concluded, Kay and I stopped off at the local Chinese takeaway to get some food for us and the kids.

To our surprise, we bumped into Kay's cousin and he was as surprised to see us as we were to see him. He asked us what we were doing there. When we explained about the project and mentioned who we were working with, Kay's cousin shared his thoughts with us about our choice of partners. With the most colorful language possible, he left no doubts that we were working with someone of less than reputable worth. "Count the fingers on your hand after you shake his," was the parting wisdom that he gave me.

Less than a week later, I happened to mention the name of our developer with a business acquaintance. I thought that they might be a good networking connection for a new business networking group that was being set up south of Auckland. Once again, the feedback that we received was less than favourable.

Yet, despite the 'writing on the wall', we decided to proceed with this business venture.

Unfortunately, our developers faced their own financial crisis and they eventually had to put the business into receivership. We ended up losing money in the project as tasks that we had paid for were not completed.

After a discussion with the liquidators, our partially completed project was passed to another developer, who we contracted to complete the project within the same scope and costs as our original developers.

Once again, messages returned to us about the new developers and their less than perfect reputation. Within six months, they too went into voluntary liquidation, having embezzled over $100,000 of our hard-earned cash.

By now we had accumulated nearly $2,000,000 of debt and we still needed in excess of $160,000 to complete the project. We had reached the absolute limit of what the bank would loan us, and the well was dry. It proved to be a particularly stressful time for both Kay and me.

WHAT IS THE WRITING ON THE WALL?

The only thing that we both knew to do was to lean into God. We needed to fast and pray for Him to do one of His many miracles.

This reminds me of the story about the Christian who is talking to God. Feeling that he has a good relationship with God, the Christian asks, "God what is a million dollars to You?"

God replies, "It's like a penny to Me."

Encouraged by what he hears, the Christian asks another question. "And what is a million years like to You?"

"It's just a second," God replies.

With his courage built up, the Christian tries his hand with a final question, "God, can I please have a million dollars?"

"Sure," God replies. "Just wait a second!"

We waited for what seemed like a million years before God came through.

Through the hard work of our accountant, we avoided paying a hefty tax bill. We managed to sell off a partially built house. We cleared a large mountain of debt when the title of the four properties were successfully sold off and we even found a new owner of the original house in the corner of this subdivision. But that still left us with over $1,050,000 of debt.

The final piece in the puzzle manifested itself in the sale of the first investment property that we owned. Purchased in 2009, during the height of the GFC, the property had increased significantly in value.

By the end of 2017, Kay and I approached our rental manager and a Realtor that we trusted to discuss the best timing to sell that property. We agreed that giving the tenant notice that we wanted to sell just before Christmas, was not the right thing to do. The potential stress that we would put on them was unacceptable. Instead, we chose the first week in January to tell them.

Realizing that they controlled the timing of their departure from the property, we knew that the potential worst-case scenario was that the house would be empty 90 days from the day we gave them notice. Maybe, if we were lucky, they might agree to move out earlier if they found alternative rental accommodation.

In our case, thankfully it was around the end of January 2018 that the tenants gave us their notice and we knew that we could put the property on the open market. It was pleasantly sooner than we anticipated.

With this knowledge, we arranged to meet the Realtor at the property on Monday the 19th of February, with the agreement of the tenants. This was a week before they vacated the property. Armed with a tape measure, pen, and paper, we walked through the property and detailed the work required to renovate the house with the purpose of maximizing the value at auction.

The list of works grew. We needed to change the carpets and paint the walls. The garden needed maintenance. Decking needed replacement and uneven ground needed repair. As the list grew, so did the cost. I had an acquaintance from one of my business networking groups come over to deliver a quote for the remedial work. The cost exceeded $47,000. This was money that we didn't have.

Our Realtor worked through her rolodex and identified tradies (some would call them contractors) that she had used to quote for the painting; the carpet; the carpentry; even the staging. Soon the alternative quotes brought down the investment to $30,993. Even that was outside of our financial grasp. Yet, we agreed to proceed. I had to have the faith to hand this over to God and know that He was going to underwrite the cheques for us. I knew that I was about to start leveraging God again.

The tenants vacated on the 25th of February and the tradies started arriving the following morning.

By this stage, I was already committed to organizing a conference called the Global Speakers Summit (2018) which we were hosting at the Sky City Convention Centre. As I left the property, my focus shifted to the responsibility of leading the Global Speakers Summit, greeting our guests and delivering the largest gathering of thought leaders in New Zealand in the last five years. My only connection to the renovation was the payment of invoices as they rolled in.

Within a week we had completely renovated the property. With the smell of fresh paint and new carpets, the property was staged and the photographer arrived to take the snaps that would be used to fuel the auction process. The property went live on the market and the Realtor controlled the process with

WHAT IS THE WRITING ON THE WALL?

the concentrated precision of an orchestral conductor.

The auction was set for the 26th of March. We had three weeks to market the property and gain interest from potential bidders.

To our pleasure, the Realtor contacted us with some good news on the 14th of March. We had received a pre-auction offer of $820,000. Whilst it wasn't at the level that we were seeking for the sale, it brought us to within $230,000 of clearing our debt.

As Kay and I discussed this offer, I was reminded that when we purchased our house, we were told that the auctioneers opening bid would be $100,000 below the reserve. So asking or receiving $920,000 would be a God thing.

Kay and I signed the pre-auction offer the following day and that evening I boarded a plane to fly to Brisbane, where I was speaking at another conference.

Because of the pre-auction offer, we were able to pull forward the date of the auction. It was now reset to Monday the 19th of March.

TIME TO REFLECT...

What are some of the learning lessons in this experience?

This was another case of God having a loophole for us. We purchased a property in 2009, at the height of the GFC, but God had predestined for us to own it so that we can sell it in 2018 to cover most of our debt.

Working with our Realtor, we received favor in the quotes to have the work done, shaving over $16,000 off our bill.

I was able to focus on delivering a successful conference because I wasn't worried about the house. God had my back!

CHAPTER EIGHTEEN

Are you ready to start bidding?

Being in Brisbane, I needed a way to communicate with Kay, who was attending the auction with our daughter Brianna. Eventually, we decided to use WhatsApp

> *HI Dad Were at the auction will tell you about the bids* 😊
> [16:57, 19/03/2018] Brianna Kanaris:
>
> *Thanks. Just txt the number e.g. 868 = $868K 899 = $899K etc*
> [16:59, 19/03/2018] Elias Kanaris:
>
> *Yup got it*
> [16:59, 19/03/2018] Brianna Kanaris:
>
> *Mum told me the same thing. Wow what faith in me. Need I remind you that one of us is a teenager, we invented the abbreviations abbr for short* 😊😂
> [17:00, 19/03/2018] Brianna Kanaris:

♥️😁

[17:01, 19/03/2018] Elias Kanaris:

Starting

[17:01, 19/03/2018] Brianna Kanaris:

875

[17:05, 19/03/2018] Brianna Kanaris:

😁

[17:05, 19/03/2018] Elias Kanaris:

880

[17:05, 19/03/2018] Brianna Kanaris:

885

[17:05, 19/03/2018] Brianna Kanaris:

👍

[17:06, 19/03/2018] Elias Kanaris:

895

[17:06, 19/03/2018] Brianna Kanaris:

900

[17:06, 19/03/2018] Brianna Kanaris:

👍😁

[17:06, 19/03/2018] Elias Kanaris:

905

[17:06, 19/03/2018] Brianna Kanaris:

👍

[17:06, 19/03/2018] Elias Kanaris:

ARE YOU READY TO START BIDDING?

907
[17:06, 19/03/2018] Brianna Kanaris:

909
[17:06, 19/03/2018] Brianna Kanaris:

910
[17:06, 19/03/2018] Brianna Kanaris:

👍
[17:06, 19/03/2018] Elias Kanaris:

912
[17:07, 19/03/2018] Brianna Kanaris:

915
[17:07, 19/03/2018] Brianna Kanaris:

👍
[17:07, 19/03/2018] Elias Kanaris:

917
[17:07, 19/03/2018] Brianna Kanaris:

920
[17:07, 19/03/2018] Brianna Kanaris:

😀
[17:07, 19/03/2018] Elias Kanaris:

921
[17:07, 19/03/2018] Brianna Kanaris:

925
[17:07, 19/03/2018] Brianna Kanaris:

927

[17:07, 19/03/2018] Brianna Kanaris:

👍

[17:08, 19/03/2018] Elias Kanaris:

933

[17:08, 19/03/2018] Brianna Kanaris:

😀😀😀😀

[17:08, 19/03/2018] Elias Kanaris:

936

[17:08, 19/03/2018] Brianna Kanaris:

940

[17:08, 19/03/2018] Brianna Kanaris:

942

[17:08, 19/03/2018] Brianna Kanaris:

👍😀

[17:08, 19/03/2018] Elias Kanaris:

947

[17:08, 19/03/2018] Brianna Kanaris:

949

[17:09, 19/03/2018] Brianna Kanaris:

👍😀

[17:09, 19/03/2018] Elias Kanaris:

950

[17:09, 19/03/2018] Brianna Kanaris:

Beauty
[17:09, 19/03/2018] Elias Kanaris:

And sold!!
[17:09, 19/03/2018] Brianna Kanaris:

[17:10, 19/03/2018] Elias Kanaris:

How awesome is that!!! PTL. For His generosity
[17:10, 19/03/2018] Elias Kanaris:

Uncle David apparently said that we'd get 950 for it a couple of days ago
[17:11, 19/03/2018] Brianna Kanaris:

Since when did he become a property magnate? He should have said $1M
[17:11, 19/03/2018] Elias Kanaris:

And, at the drop of a hammer, we managed to reduce our debt, shrinking it down to $106,000! Less than six months earlier we had been staring down the double-barrels of $2,000,000 of debt.

Because the sale was made through an auction, we received the deposit minus the Realtors' commission 10 working days after the auction, which gave us enough cash to tide us over and pay the outstanding invoices.

If I had the eyes of a worldly-view, I might have called it a day when we were still $2,000,000 in debt. Going into voluntary liquidation might have seemed like the ONLY option. Yet, with NO ability to borrow any money and with bills coming in, we had to draw on our faith in God.

We had leaned into the Word of God.

> [1]*"Praise the Lord.*
> *Blessed are those who fear the Lord,*

> *who find great delight in his commands.*
> *² Their children will be mighty in the land;*
> *the generation of the upright will be blessed.*
> *³ Wealth and riches are in their houses,*
> *and their righteousness endures forever."*
> (Psalm 112:1-3, NKJV)

Wealth and riches will be in my house and I will be blessed! Why? Because I fear the LORD and I delight in His commandments.

I know that I need to keep myself grounded. The reason that I'm successful is NOT because of me, but because of HIM in me.

There is a story in the Old Testament, in 1 Chronicles, Chapter 5, that details the genealogical records that were taken during the reigns of Jotham, king of Judah, and Jeroboam, king of Israel. It states that there were 44,760 men ready for military service from the tribe of the Reubenites, the Gadites and the half-tribe of Manasseh.

They waged war against the Hagrites, Jetur, Naphish, and Nodab. And they won!

> *"They were helped in fighting them, and God delivered the Hagrites and all their allies into their hands, because they cried out to him during the battle. He answered their prayers, because they trusted in him."*
> (1 Chronicles 5:20, NIV)

I found out that you can call out to God at ANY time – even in the middle of the battle! He will heed my prayer because He knows that I trust Him!

What battle are you waging now? What do you need to cry out to God for to help deliver you out of your current situation? When I find myself in trouble, I know that God (and my situation) is only a prayer away. I need not worry.

TIME TO REFLECT...

What are some of the learning lessons in this experience?

God is listening to our prayers.

All we have to do is ask, and it shall be given to us; pressed down, shaken together and running over! And I have to trust Him! Unconditionally!!

LEVERAGING GOD

CHAPTER NINETEEN

Conclusion

Was I really the accidental President? As I look back, I can see that this was no accident.

God had predestined me to become the President of the Global Speakers Federation. He had created me for a time like this. A time to bring His people back from the wilderness and to deliver them to arise from another place.

In his letter to the Romans, the apostle Paul lays out the major themes of sin, salvation, redemption, justification, grace, and reconciliation. Because Paul is such an outstanding teaching-leader, he communicates with purpose. He doesn't just attempt to inform – he goes the extra mile and seeks to transform the Church that he's writing to.

After he spends the first chapter building a rapport with this Church, Paul spends the next chapter creating a dilemma relevant to everyone. Reminding them that God spoke, creating mankind and the human conscience into existence, he then brings to the reader's attention the predicament of sin and its impact on mankind.

He contrasts how man tries to make everything right on his own, but never succeeds. Paul shares that it is God's gift of righteousness that we can only receive through faith. And it is that faith, mixed with the grace that God gave us, through the sacrifice of Jesus on the cross for our sins, that wins our redemption.

> [28] *"And we know that in all things God works for the good of those who love him, who have been called according to his purpose.*
> [29] *For those God foreknew he also predestined to be conformed to the image of his Son, that he might be the firstborn among many brothers and sisters.* [30]*And those he predestined, he also called; those he called, he also justified; those he justified, he also glorified."*
> (Romans 8:28-30, NIV)

God foreknew about me. He called me. He predestined me to be conformed in the image of His Son. He made me firstborn amongst many brothers and sisters.

Whom he called; he justified.

Whom he justified; he also GLORIFIED!

It has always been my prayer that you, the reader, would receive some insight from God and the Holy Spirit that would help you in your spiritual journey. Whether you are a new Christian, a mature believer; someone who has no faith or a person whose faith has lapsed, there is a pathway that God has created for you.

The best advice that I received when I started my Speaking business was to attend as many events and offer to serve. I will encourage you to give. At your Church. In your community. At work.

> *"Give, and it will be given to you. A good measure, pressed down, shaken together and running over, will be poured into your lap. For with the measure you use, it will be measured to you."*
> (Luke 6:38, NIV)

When you start leveraging God, you start to multiply your efforts. The fruit will be bountiful.

CONCLUSION

To help you on your journey, let me recommend that you do three things:

1) Get a copy of the Bible and start to read it. God has written His story for you to read. If you haven't read the Bible before, start off with the four gospels (Matthew, Mark, Luke, and John) that start the New Testament. Once you are more confident, maybe you can read a chapter of Proverbs each day. Since there are 31 Chapters in Proverbs, that means that you can cycle through the book of Proverbs each month. This is God's way of speaking to you.
2) Start to pray. Prayer is our way of talking to God. I'm not sure what your concept of prayer is, but there is no magic bullet when it comes to prayer. For me, and many others, the best form of prayer is the same as having a candid conversation with your spouse. There is a great book called "Conversations with God" by Neale Donald Walsch which I would recommend that you read.
3) Find a good Church to attend. We all need shelter and a Church is a great place to start. It provides you with the refuge from the storm that may be playing out in your life. At a good Church, you will be able to find community and maybe, like me, the equivalent to our Gateway program. This way you can get answers to some of your questions.

What is your given name? How has it been used to hold you back? (Or, more importantly, what have you believed that has held you back?) No matter what others have spoken over your name, take the time to find Your Secret Name.

I have been called by the caller. God is the author and perfecter. He doesn't make mistakes and I need to accept that I am made in His image.

As I review the journey that God has taken me through, I can see how and why the enemy has been so keen to derail me. The lies came at me from an early age. But I was named before conception. God had already picked out my identity before I was knitted in my mother's womb.

He has blessed me and taken care of my every need. He knows every hair on my head and the need of the sparrow. He will continue to provide. And, as I step into my faith and become more Christ-like, I will continue to reap the bountiful rewards that He has stored for me to enjoy here on earth as it is in heaven.

So, if God is speaking to you, what is He saying? And what are you doing to obey him?

As soon as the thought left my brain, I heard God speak. "Elias, it's time for you to take over the stage..."

LEVERAGING GOD

A FINAL NOTE

Strengthen yourself to achieve anything you desire

Now that you have finished reading this book, what are you going to do? What actions are you going to take? Which self-limiting beliefs are you going to change? Which Given Name are you going to discard? When are you going to pick up your Bible and have an honest and frank conversation with God?

How are you going to impact yourself, your family, team, organisation, or country?

As I said in the introduction, this book is not about manipulating God. It is about partnering with Him and leveraging His strength to compensate for your weakness. It's about using the principle of leverage to your advantage. A lever works by reducing the amount of force needed to move an object or lift a load. A lever does this by increasing the distance through which the force acts.

I love the scripture in Ephesians 3:20. It states:

> "Now to Him who is able to do exceedingly abundantly above all that we ask or think, according to the power that works in us"
> (Ephesians 3:20, NKJV)

I deliberately chose the NKJV (New King James Version) of this scripture, because this is the version that I first read in my Maxwell Leadership Bible. I was so excited when I read this that I ran to Kay and told her that "God can do exceedingly abundantly above all that we ask or think."

Kay's first reaction was to tell me that that was grammatically incorrect. There was no such phrase as "exceedingly abundantly". Let me tell you, it gave me great pleasure to give her my copy of the Bible for her to read the scripture. To make it even easier, I had highlighted the scripture with a yellow highlighter!

Let me help you break this scripture down...

The 'Him' that this scripture is referring to is God.

He can do 'exceedingly abundantly'. Not just abundantly, but exceedingly abundantly. Can you try to get your head around that? I know that I am still trying to fathom the depth and the width and the height of what He is able to do. Honestly, I would have been happy with abundantly. But, apparently, I have to do with exceedingly abundantly!

Oh, and that doesn't include the next word – 'above'.

This means 'more than'.

"...above all that we ask or think..." What are you asking for and thinking about?

Let me pause here. I would like you to consider the following. I believe that the concept of 'asking' can be related to the act of 'praying'. For me, prayer is a simple act of talking to God. It would be the same as me talking to you, or you talking to somebody else who is a big part of your life. I remember Kay telling me once that she had been 'talking to God' when she was walking along the beach. It was related to her taking a particular job that she had applied for. Like me, she was waiting for the H.R. team to respond with a job offer and she was asking God why there was a delay. And what did God say to Kay? "I'm waiting to get my ducks in a row!" (Trust me, this is what He said!)

I'm not sure how God talks to you. He may be as down to earth as he was with Kay. Or He could be more direct as He is with me. "God, I was thinking of making a $10,000 donation to this offering. What do You think?" His response can be a simple grunt or a "Yep!"

'Thinking', on the other hand, I believe is related to your faith. Do you have faith that God can do things or not? If you analyze this scripture, it tells us

A FINAL NOTE

that He will give us exceedingly abundantly above all that we "ask or think". So is what you are asking for aligning with what you are thinking?

If you ask for one thing, but think, "You know what, I don't think that I can get that," why would you expect God to work His miracles to deliver what you are asking for? I believe that He is asking for you to have the same amount of faith to ask for something specific. Try aligning your thinking (faith) with your asking (prayer).

If this was the end of the scripture, then we can all go away happy and content that things will change for the better. But that isn't the end of the verse. There are eight, small, but very powerful, words that follow... "...according to the power that works within us."

Think about that. What if God has already put in place all the power that you will need to make this happen? Wow! Now you're cooking with gas!

I believe that He has. Before Jesus was crucified, He spoke with His disciples. He told them of a 'Helper' who would be coming:

> *"But the Helper, the Holy Spirit, whom the Father will send in My name, He will teach you all things, and bring to your remembrance all things that I said to you."*
> (John 14:26, NKJV)

After His resurrection, Jesus walked the earth for forty days. He again reminded his disciples that He would send His Helper. On the day of Pentecost, the Holy Spirit came:

> [1]*"When the day of Pentecost came, they were all together in one place.* [2]*Suddenly a sound like the blowing of a violent wind came from heaven and filled the whole house where they were sitting.* [3]*They saw what seemed to be tongues of fire that separated and came to rest on each of them.* [4]*All of them were filled with the Holy Spirit and began to speak in other tongues as the Spirit enabled them."*
> (Acts 2:1-4, NIV)

To help you understand how you can start leveraging God, let me encourage you to take the first step and invite Jesus into your heart. It is something that Kay and I were invited to do when we attended that Church service during that January evening in 2005. As the Pastor encouraged us to do that day, I encourage you to do the same. Invite Jesus into your heart by sharing this prayer:

> "Lord Jesus, for too long I've kept You out of my life. I know that I am a sinner and that I cannot save myself. No longer will I close the door when I hear You knocking. Thank You, Lord Jesus, for coming to Earth. I believe You are the Son of God who died on the cross for my sins and rose from the dead on the third day. By faith, I gratefully receive Your gift of salvation. I am ready to trust You as my Lord and Saviour. Thank You for bearing my sins and giving me the gift of eternal life. Come into my heart, Lord Jesus, and be my Savior. Amen."

I wish you all the best as you start your personal journey. Use this book as a self-leadership road map of personal transformation. I pray that you can understand the power of leveraging God and how that will start giving you strength to help you achieve anything you desire.

ABOUT THE AUTHOR

ELIAS KANARIS is an author, professional keynote speaker, executive coach, leadership trainer, and entrepreneur. He has been a regular keynote presenter and he has frequently spoken to audiences in the I.T., telecommunications, insurance, financial services, real estate, and education sectors across thirteen countries on four continents. Since the early 1980s, Elias has been using humor and energy to deliver great learning experiences to his audiences. He published his first book, 'Liberating Your Leadership Potential: Changing self-limiting beliefs to lead your team, organization or country with influence' in 2016. His articles have been published in Lead, Market$hare Magazine, New Inceptions, and Leadership Inspirational Magazine.

Elias has a Master in Science in Medical Electronics from the University of Wales, Institute of Science and Technology (UWIST), and he has a Bachelor's Degree in Electrical and Electronic Engineering from Kingston University.

He has been a senior consultant in the I.T. and Telecommunications sector, where he was part of a team responsible for his company's top twenty-four clients, which billed $450 million per annum. Elias is also a founding partner of the John Maxwell Team (JMT) – the largest and fastest-growing leadership training organization in the world. He has served as a member of the President's Advisory Council (PAC) and was a founding member of the Peer Review Team on the JMT. Elias served as the National President for the Professional Speakers Association of New Zealand (2015-2017). He also served as President of the Global Speakers Federation (2018-2019), a $4 Billion industry that represents Professional Speakers globally.

Elias was born in North Africa, was educated in the UK, and now lives in Murrays Bay in Auckland, New Zealand. He lives within five minutes walking distance from a beach and enjoys the lifestyle most people dreamt about in their youth.

ABOUT EXECUTIVE COACHING

Research from the International Coach Federation indicates that professional coaching brings many wonderful benefits, including marked increases in productivity and a range of interpersonal skills that lead to increased customer satisfaction and a strong return on investment.

People who are coached comment that they get fresh perspectives on personal challenges, enhanced decision-making skills, greater interpersonal effectiveness, and increased confidence. And the list does not end there. Those who undertake coaching can also expect appreciable improvement in productivity, satisfaction with life and work, and the attainment of relevant goals.

Professional coaching maximizes potential and, therefore, unlocks latent sources of productivity. Research from the International Coaching Federation (http://italentia.com/excellence-through-improved-thinking/) shows that coaching:

- Improves work performance by 70 percent
- Increases business management by 61 percent
- Improves time management by 57 percent
- Improves team effectiveness by 51 percent

Building employees' self-confidence so they can face challenges is critical in meeting organizational demands. By investing in an executive coach, it has been shown that:

- Self-confidence can be increased by 80 percent
- Relationships can be improved by 73 percent
- Communications skills can be improved by 72 percent
- Life/Work balance can be improved by 67 percent

Executive coaching generates learning and clarity for forward action with a commitment to measurable outcomes. The vast majority of companies (86 percent) say they at least earned back their investments.

I have been supplying executive coaching services since 2011, and I have provided thousands of hours of coaching to clients across the manufacturing, insurance, financial services, direct marketing, telecommunications, and real-estate industries. I have helped my clients to qualify for MDRT (Million Dollar Round Table), achieve their business and personal goals, and become better organized.

Virtually, all companies and individuals who hire a coach are satisfied. Altogether, 99 percent have been "Somewhat" or "Very Satisfied" with their overall experience, and 96 percent claimed they would repeat the process.

If you are serious about making a change in your life, I would love to be part of your journey. As a Christian in business, I know that things can be tough. The scriptures have taught me that one can put aside a thousand, and two can put aside ten thousand. But a triple-braided cord cannot be broken. I know that walking alone is difficult in business. I would encourage you to look for your local Lifework Leadership program and consider investing in yourself.

Lifework Leadership is about becoming a City Changer. It's about taking the Jesus Journey.

For more information about my executive coaching services, visit one of my websites listed below and then text me your name, time zone, and the best time to redeem a 30-60 minute, no-obligation, executive coaching consultation by phone, Skype, or Zoom call.

www.EliasKanaris.com

www.LeveragingGod.com

www.LiberatingYourLeadershipPotential.com

www.LifeworkLeadership.nz

Phone: +64 (0) 9 280 4420

BOOK ELIAS KANARIS TO SPEAK AT YOUR NEXT EVENT

When it comes to choosing a professional speaker for your next event, you will find no one more respected or successful – no one who will leave your audience or colleagues with a more renewed passion for life – than Elias Kanaris, one of the most gifted speakers of our generation. Since 1986, Elias Kanaris has delivered more than 2,000 inspirational presentations worldwide.

Whether your audience is 10 or 10,000 in New Zealand or abroad, Elias Kanaris can deliver a customized message of inspiration for your congregation, meeting or conference. Elias understands that your audience does not want to be "taught" anything, but is rather interested in hearing stories of inspiration, achievement, and real-life people liberating their leadership potential. He is as comfortable in a corporate environment, the boardroom or the Church.

As a result, Elias Kanaris' speaking philosophy is to humor, entertain, and inspire your audience with passion and stories proven to help people achieve extraordinary results. If you are looking for a memorable speaker who will leave your audience wanting more, book Elias Kanaris today!

To see a highlight video of Elias Kanaris and find out whether he is available for your next meeting, visit his website at the address below. Then contact him by phone or email to schedule a pre-keynote phone interview:

www.EliasKanaris.com
Elias@EliasKanaris.com

www.ReduceDebt.nz
Phone: +64 (0) 9 280 4420

Unless otherwise noted, all Scripture quotations are taken from the New King James Version®. Copyright © 1982 by Thomas Nelson. Used by permission. All rights reserved. Scripture quotations marked AMP are taken from the Amplified® Bible, copyright © 1954, 1987 by The Lockman Foundation. Used by permission. (www.Lockman.org); ESV are taken from the ESV® Bible (The Holy Bible, English Standard Version®), copyright © 2001 by Crossway, a publishing ministry of Good News Publishers. Used by permission. All rights reserved; HCSB are taken from the Holman Christian Standard Bible®, copyright © 1999, 2003 by Holman Bible Publishers. Used by permission. Holman Christian Standard Bible®, Holman CSB®, and HCSB® are federally registered trademarks of Holman Bible Publishers; TLB are taken from The Living Bible, copyright © 1971. Used by permission of Tyndale House Publishers, Inc., Carol Stream, Illinois 60188. All rights reserved; THE MESSAGE are taken from THE MESSAGE. Copyright © by Eugene H. Peterson 1993, 2002. Used by permission of Tyndale House Publishers, Inc.; NASB are taken from the New American Standard Bible®, copyright © 1960, 1995 by The Lockman Foundation. Used by permission. (www.Lockman.org); NIV are taken from the Holy Bible, NEW INTERNATIONAL VERSION®, NIV. Copyright © 1973, 2011 by Biblica, Inc.® Used by permission. All rights reserved worldwide. NEW INTERNATIONAL VERSION® and NIV® are registered trademarks of Biblica, Inc. Use of either trademark for the offering of goods or services requires the prior written consent of Biblica, Inc.; NLT are taken from the Holy Bible, New Living Translation, copyright © 1996, 2007 by Tyndale House Foundation. Used by permission of Tyndale House Publishers, Inc., Carol Stream, Illinois 60188. All rights reserved; PHILLIPS are taken from The New Testament in Modern English, Revised Edition © 1972 by J. B. Phillips. Copyright renewed © 1986, 1988 by Vera M. Phillips. The author has added italics to Scripture quotations for emphasis.

www.ingramcontent.com/pod-product-compliance
Lightning Source LLC
Chambersburg PA
CBHW072005110526
44592CB00012B/1213